Tips and Traps for Saving on <u>All</u> Your Real Estate Taxes

Other McGraw-Hill Books by Robert Irwin

Tips and Traps for Saving on <u>All</u> Your Real Estate Taxes

Robert Irwin

Norman Lane

McGraw-Hill, Inc.

New York   San Francisco   Washington, D.C.   Auckland   Bogotá
Caracas   Lisbon   London   Madrid   Mexico City   Milan
Montreal   New Delhi   San Juan   Singapore
Sydney   Tokyo   Toronto

Library of Congress Cataloging-in-Publication Data

Irwin, Robert (date.)
    Tips and traps for saving on all your real estate taxes / Robert Irwin, Norman Lane.
        p.   cm.
    Includes index.
    ISBN 0-07-032395-X — ISBN 0-07-032396-8 (pbk.)
    1. Real property and taxation—United States—Popular works.
    2. Real estate investment—Taxation—Law and legislation—United States—Popular
works. I. Lane, Norman H. II. Title.
    KF6540.Z9I78   1994
    343.7305'46—dc20
    [347.303546]   93-23551
                                                                    CIP

1 2 3 4 5 6 7 8 9 0   DOC/DOC   9 9 8 7 6 5 4 3

ISBN 0-07-032396-8 (pbk)
ISBN 0-07-032395-X (hc)

The sponsoring editor for this book was James H. Bessent, Jr., the editing
supervisor was Nancy Young, and the production supervisor was Donald F.
Schmidt. This book was set in Palatino. It was composed by Karen Calise.

Printed and bound by R. R. Donnelley & Sons Company.

Contents

---

viii Contents

11. How to Reduce Property Taxes — 125

How Property Taxes Are Levied 126
Evaluating Individual Properties 128
The Tax Rule 129
Tying the Hands of Government 130
Challenging Your Property Taxes 131
Reassessments Caused by Improvements 141
When You Improve More Than Half the Value of the Property 143

12. Real Estate Tax Planning Strategies — 145

Time Line 146
Strategies When Purchasing 147
Economics versus Tax Benefits 150
Taking Title 152
Strategies during Ownership 155
Strategies When Selling 157
All-Purpose Strategies 160

13. Record Keeping — 163

What Is a Record? 164
Where to Keep Your Records 167
Records that You Will Want to Keep 168

14. Capital Gains and Losses — 171

Capital Losses 172
Future Changes 174
Foreign Owners 174
Imputed Interest 175

Appendix A. Tax Credits — 177

Appendix B. Major Changes Made by the 1993 Tax Law — 181

Appendix C. Tax Forms — 183

Index 203

Preface

The real reason that I wanted to write this book is that I've always wanted to read it. I've needed a good authoritative source that was easy to read to answer my real estate tax questions. While I like to think I've got a pretty good command of the tax rules, I've found it impossible to keep all the technicalities in my head. I always needed a quick reference to grab when a question came up.

Not finding anything really suitable in the marketplace, I began jotting down notes here and there—some fine points on tax-free exchanges, the exact rules for the once-in-a-lifetime $125,000 exclusion, the applications of the installment sale, and so on.

It worked, sort of, but a book would be far better. So when McGraw-Hill began looking for a new topic for the highly successful "Tips and Traps" series, I naturally suggested real estate taxes—a book that could fill a real need.

The trouble is that while I consider myself an expert on real estate, I don't really feel like a sufficient enough expert on real estate taxes to write a whole book about the subject. So, I asked my good friend, Norman Lane, if he would write it with me.

Norman is the ideal person with whom to write a book on real estate taxes. He's an attorney, Harvard educated. He was a full professor of tax law at USC (held the Milliken Professorship

of Taxation). He was even a law clerk for the Honorable
Thurgood Marshall when he served as a judge of the U.S. Court
of Appeals, Second Circuit.

Norman liked the idea, only now he's a partner in the
national and international law firm of Bryan Cave, where he
heads up their West Coast tax practice. How could he find the
time to do his regular work *and* write a tax book?

Norman said he probably couldn't. But, since he's a very old
friend, I impressed the need upon him, and he finally relented.
He would try.

The result is this book. But, doing it almost killed both of us. I
pride myself in getting manuscripts in on time, but with
Norman's tight schedule and my other commitments, it was
almost 6 months late in the making (which, probably makes it a
better book since it's more timely—incorporating the 1993 tax
law changes).

I think this book really will help with all your real estate tax
questions. We have tried to make it as authoritative as possible,
while keeping the explanations at a level at which everyone can
understand them. Did we succeed?

All I can tell you is that now I use it as my own personal real
estate tax reference book.

Robert Irwin

Introduction

Almost anything and everything you can imagine in this country is subject to a tax of one kind or another. When you buy gasoline at the pump, you pay federal and state tax on each gallon. When you earn income from your employment, you may be subject to local as well as federal and state taxes. When you sell a property for gain, you will probably owe taxes on that sale.

There are, however, certain parts of the federal tax code that allow you to "exclude" or in some cases "defer" the payment of certain taxes. Further, taxes are not all paid at the same rate. Sometimes, while you must still pay, you may be able to pay at a lower rate. And finally, the tax code is constantly changed by Congress and by the decisions of various courts as well as by rules adopted by the Internal Revenue Service. Thus, what you may not have to pay tax on today, you might have to pay on tomorrow. And that could change again the day after.

If that all sounds confusing, rest assured, it is! However, it is also possible to understand it, with a little help. In this book we are going to concentrate on the federal income taxes involved with real estate. We are going to attempt to explain them as they are when this is written, with the understanding that they could be changed later on, perhaps even by the time that you read this. Further, we are going to make an effort to show you how to pay the least amount of tax possible.

It's important to understand, however, that we do not intend

to propose or suggest that you do anything illegal or even ques-
tionable when it comes to tax avoidance. Rather, our intention is
to point out how you may reduce your tax burden by better
understanding the tax code and any benefits it may offer you.

   Indeed, in your particular financial position, there may be no
benefits at all available. On the other hand, with a little bit of
planning, a sizable tax savings might be obtained.

1
Excluding and Deferring

In this chapter we are going to consider two words which usually translate into tax savings: "exclusion" and "deferral."

Exclusion

The word "exclusion" means to shut out, leave out, or exclude. With regard to taxation, it means any money that you can leave out or exclude from your gross income.

Perhaps an example will be helpful in making this more understandable. Let's say that you have a vacation home which you use part of the time and which you rent out part of the time. In general, if other rules are followed, if you rent out the vacation home to others for 14 days or less each year, you can exclude the rental income you receive. In other words you can receive the income, let's say it's $500 or $1000 a week. Yet, you may exclude or leave it out when calculating your gross income. (We'll have much more to say about this in a later chapter.)

Tip

Exclusions are very desirable. You want to take advantage of them whenever possible. The tax law has a few which relate specifically to real estate and which allow you to reduce your tax bills.

Trap

Exclusions are usually subject to very specific and strict rules. In our example, you must not rent the property out for more than 14 days to get the exclusion. Rent it out for 15 days and you must then report *all* your receipts as gross income. You lose the entire benefit of the exclusion. Follow the rules precisely, or you could be the loser.

Throughout this book, we will point out a number of exclusions that may apply to you. If they do, you would be wise to spend some time researching them to determine if, indeed, you are in a position to take advantage of them.

Deferral

Deferral of gain is a little trickier to understand. Put most simply, it means that while you may realize a gain on the sale of a piece of real estate, you don't recognize that gain as taxable until a later date, usually years later. In other words, you put off until tomorrow what you would otherwise pay tax on today.

Trap

It's important to understand that with a deferral, the tax is not forgiven, overlooked, excluded, or in any way forgotten. You still owe the money. The only difference is that instead of paying it today, you end up paying it tomorrow.

Tip

The advantage of deferral is that by tomorrow you may be in a lower tax bracket or the tax laws may have changed allowing more lenient treatment in your case or you may simply be more able to pay. Unfortunately, the opposite may also occur.

Perhaps another example will help, here. Let's say that you sell your personal residence and, within 2 years, buy a new personal residence for more than the selling price of your old one. Provided you meet other strict rules (described in detail in Chapter 4), you may "defer the gain" realized on the sale of your old property. Through a careful formula, also discussed in Chapter 4, that gain is carried forward into your new personal residence.

You do not have to recognize and pay tax on the gain you made by selling your old personal residence until you sell your new personal residence. And even then, you may be able to roll it over or defer it yet again and continue doing so almost indefinitely.

To take a specific example, let's say you sold your old house for $150,000 and realized a gain of $75,000. Normally, you would recognize that gain and pay tax on the $75,000. The tax would undoubtedly be a sizable amount.

However, instead you buy a new house for $200,000 (and follow all the rules described in Chapter 4). The $75,000 gain realized on the sale of your old house is deferred, or rolled over, into your new house. You don't recognize the gain or pay tax on it, *now*. Eventually, of course, when you sell the new house, you will have to pay tax on the $75,000 gain realized from the sale of the old house (unless you again defer by buying yet another new house). Ultimately, if you die, the gain may be avoided entirely since your heirs will get the property at a "stepped-up" (current value) basis.

Deferral is simply putting off until the future the tax on gain you realize today. For some of us, that future is put off indefinitely by continued rollovers.

Tip

Two important words to understand are gain "realized" and gain "recognized." Realized gain refers to the gain you actually made on the sale or exchange of property. Recognized gain refers to the amount of realized gain that you must include in your taxable income and pay tax on. Deferral, here, means not recognizing (including in your taxable income) the gain you realized on the sale of a piece of property.

The more exclusions and deferrals you have, the less in taxes you will have to pay in any given year. However, while exclusions eliminate the tax, as noted, deferrals only move the tax burden forward; they don't eliminate it. Beware of avoiding taxes this year only to get caught with a big tax bite down the road.

Capital Gains

A capital gain (or capital loss), naturally enough, comes as a result of the sale or exchange of a capital asset, such as real estate. When you have an investment property and you sell or exchange it, you will show either a capital gain or a capital loss. (It's most unlikely you will break exactly even.)

In the next chapter we'll go into how capital gains and losses are calculated. But for now, let's just distinguish them from other kinds of income. For example, earned income or that which you make while working on your job is *not* a capital gain. Neither is interest income, such as that which is received from the bank or savings and loan on your deposits.

Capital gain is exclusive to capital, in our case, to real property. It is the gain that results from the sale or exchange of that property.

Tip

As noted earlier, sometimes the recognition of gain realized in a sale, as in that of a personal residence, may be deferred to a later date. That does not mean that there was no capital gain. Only that the tax upon it was deferred.

In the past, there was a special capital gains tax rate. It was significantly lower than the tax rate on ordinary income. For example, at one time, the maximum rate on ordinary income was 50 percent, but the rate on long-term capital gains was limited to 20 percent.

This lower capital gains tax rate was eliminated, for most purposes, by the Tax Reform Act of 1986. In the process, some of the advantage of owning investment real estate was also eliminated. Here's why.

When the capital gains rate is lower than the ordinary income rate, it is to the taxpayer's advantage to have as much income in capital gains and as little ordinary income as possible. In the past real estate provided a vehicle for converting high tax rate ordinary income to lower tax rate capital gains. It worked like this: An individual in a high tax bracket would buy a piece of investment property, as opposed to simply placing the same amount of money in an interest-bearing savings account.

This taxpayer would then hold the property for at least the minimum capital gains period (which varied over the years but was at least 6 months) and then sell, with luck, at a profit. The gain realized on the sale was recognized as a "capital gain" and taxed at a lower rate. On the other hand, money realized from ordinary income or from interest on savings accounts was taxed at a higher rate. Thus, investing in property had, effectively, converted income from a higher ordinary income tax rate to a lower capital gains rate.

Of course, that was in the past. It is mentioned here since a good many people not familiar with current tax codes still believe this method works today. For most people it doesn't; but high-income individuals who pay the 10 percent surcharge enacted in the 1993 tax law will benefit from the capital gains rate, which is not subject to the surcharge.

Tip

Today, a federal income tax on capital gains exists. As of this writing it is 28 percent, compared to the maximum tax rate for high-income individuals, which is higher, 36 or even 39.6 percent. Because the capital gains tax rate is left at 28 percent, and the ordinary rate raised, the advantage of real estate investing as a means of converting income from ordinary tax rates to lower capital gains tax rates could again be realized, of course, only by high-income taxpayers.

2
The Modern Concepts of Taxing the Sale of Real Estate

When you earn income, as from working for an employer, with certain limited exceptions such as employee expense allowances that are actually spent for business purposes, all that income is taxable. Determining the amount of income you receive is quite simple: It's what your employer pays you, plus the value of certain taxable "fringe benefits." At the end of the year you get a W-2 form that sets out exactly the amount you received or otherwise were considered to earn.

With real estate, however, it's more complicated. Owning a piece of real estate is more like owning a business. There's the amount that you originally put into the property. Then there's the rental income you receive and the expenses you incur each year. Finally, there's the amount you get when you sell. In order to determine what you will eventually pay taxes on, all of these items must be factored together. In this chapter we're going to see how this is done.

Tip

The tax rules differ depending on whether the property was for investment or whether it was your personal residence. Special rules apply for personal residences. Since investment real estate is mainly a business, many more items can be deducted as expenses. See Chapter 6 for more information.

Establishing a Tax Basis

In the simplest way of looking at things, the amount on which you will pay tax is the difference between the cost of the property and the sale price, less expenses. If you buy for $50,000 and sell for $100,000, chances are that you made a profit and will need to pay tax on it. However, the profit may not be $50,000. Along the way there are all sorts of expenses that you incurred which must be accounted for. These start when you purchase the property. For example, there are the costs of making the purchase itself.

Let's say that you buy a house for $100,000. As part of the purchase, you paid out the following:

Down payment

Closing costs (including title insurance, escrow, etc.)

Points on your loan (see Chapter 3)

Buyer's portion of a real estate agent's fee

The question is, what did the house actually cost you? The actual cost of the property is its "basis" or the point at which you begin for the purposes of calculating taxes.

The price was $100,000. However, there were expenses that you incurred as part of the purchase. Let's consider them one at a time.

Down Payment

A down payment is *not* an expense. It is part of your investment into the property. If you put $20,000 down and secured a new first mortgage for $80,000, your down payment was part of the purchase price as was the new mortgage to come up with the $100,000 purchase price. The relative size of the down payment compared to the amount financed by the mortgage does not affect the basis because both are considered elements of cost.

Trap

This is an important concept to grasp as we'll see later on. Often owners will refinance, taking money out of a property. By doing so they have not changed the basis. That means when it comes time to sell, their taxes may be high, but their equity (because they refinanced earlier on) may be low, resulting in a most unpleasant situation.

Closing Costs

These days it is not unusual to have thousands of dollars in closing costs. These can include title insurance, escrow charges, inspection fees, loan fees, recording fees, and on and on. These are expenses that you paid as part of the purchase that were *in addition* to the purchase price. Let's say your closing costs were $3000. In determining your tax basis, or what you paid for the property, you would add the $3000 to the price:

Price (down payment and mortgage)	$100,000
Closing costs	+3,000

Trap

Many people suppose that points paid to secure a loan are also costs of purchase and affect the basis. This is not technically accurate. Points and fees incident to obtaining a loan are amortized (spread out) over the life of the loan and written off when the loan is repaid. They don't affect the basis of the property purchased with the proceeds of the loan.

Tip

If the property you purchased was for your own personal residence and you fulfilled certain qualifications, instead of amortizing the points over the life of the loan, you may be able to deduct them from your income in the year of the purchase.

Generally speaking you can deduct points paid for the purchase of your personal residence in the year paid provided:

The loan was used to buy (or to improve) your personal residence (main home).

The points do not exceed amounts normally charged in your area and paying them is an established business practice.

The points were computed as a percentage of the mortgage amount.

You paid for the points with your own funds. In other words, you did not pay for the points out of the mortgage.

See Chapter 3 for more details.

Agent's Fees

These days it is becoming increasingly common for buyers to have their own agents. You may have had to pay a buyer's agent's fee. Let's say this fee was $1500. This also is an expense that you incurred as part of your purchase of the house.

Price (down payment and mortgage)	$100,000
Closing costs	+3,000
Buyer's agent's fee	+1,500
Basis	$104,500

Calculating the Basis

As the above calculation shows, after you have added in all your allowable costs involved in the purchase of the home, you arrive at the tax base, what you actually paid for the property, $104,500 in our example. This tax basis can change during ownership of the property for a wide variety of reasons. The following will give you some reasons the basis can be lowered or raised.

Receipts and Items That Lower Basis

Depreciation. Taken on investment real estate

Insurance reimbursement.   For a casualty loss suffered on your personal residence

Payments.   Received for the sale of a portion of the property or for easements or rights of way granted to others

Costs That Raise the Basis

Improvements.   To a personal residence or not fully depreciated for investment property

Capital expenses.   For example, costs of defending title to property

Property restoration costs.   After a casualty loss

Net Selling Price

The gain you realize on the sale of a property (and on which you will be taxed) is the difference between the basis, calculated above, and the net sales price. "Net" means the actual sales price, less allowable costs of sale. For example, if you sell your property for a sales price of $150,000, you normally do not get that amount. Instead, you have expenses involved in the sales such as agent's fees, closing costs, fix-up, etc. These expenses adjust the sales price downward. Let's see how this works:

Agent's Fee

As a seller, you can reasonably expect to hire a real estate agent to facilitate the sale of your property. The agent's fee is deductible from the proceeds of sale in computing gain.

Tip

The fee an agent charges is not set by law, trade organization, or custom. It is determined entirely by negotiation between the seller and the agent. Thus, the full amount of the agent's fee is considered an expense of the sale. Let's say it's 6 percent of the sales price. In our example, this would be $9000:

Sales price	$150,000
Agent's fee	–9,000

Closing Costs

As with a buyer, you as a seller will have many closing costs. These may include escrow and title insurance costs, home warranty protection plans, document fees, and so on. Normally these are all expenses allowed as part of the sale of the property. Let's say, in our example, that the closing costs come to an even $3000:

Sales price	$150,000
Agent's fee	–9,000
Closing costs	–3,000

Fix-Up Costs

It may be necessary for you to fix up, clean, paint, etc., your property in order to make it presentable for sale. If the home was your *personal residence* (as opposed to an investment house), expenses may be used to adjust the sales price, subject to strict limitations.

Trap

Adjustments for fix-up to a personal residence can only be used for purposes of determining how much of your gain can be deferred if you buy a new home within 2 years, as explained in the last chapter. You *cannot* use fix-up expenses to reduce the sales price if you simply sell the home outright. For the purpose of calculating the gain that will be postponed, the following rules apply:

The work was done during the 90 days *prior* to the date on the sales contract.

You pay for the work no later than 30 days after the sale.

You don't deduct the expenses elsewhere.

You don't consider the expenses a capital improvement or expenditure.

Tip

For investment property, all the costs involved in fixing up and cleaning up the property either during ownership or in preparation for sale are considered expenses for the purpose of either adjusting the sales price or determining loss.

We'll say that there were $500 in allowable fix-up costs:

Sales price	$150,000
Agent's feet	–9,000
Closing costs	–3,000
Fix-up costs	–500
Adjusted sales price	$137,500

Determining Gain Realized from the Sale of Real Estate

Once we have the tax basis of your property and the adjusted sales price, it is simply a matter of subtracting one from the other to determine the gain realized. However, it is important to remember that during the term of ownership, the basis (originally calculated at $106,500) could have changed dramatically. For example, if during part of your term of ownership, you rented the house out, you could have depreciated the structure (not the land) during that time. (See Chapter 6 for more information on depreciation.) The basis could have gone down significantly. Let's say that while you owned the house, you had depreciation during that period of $15,000; the basis therefore would be reduced by that amount:

Basis	$106,500
Depreciation over 5 years	–15,000
Adjusted basis	$ 91,500

On the other hand, you may have added a room to the property. The cost of the improvement could have been $25,000. This could be added to the basis regardless of whether it was an investment property or a personal residence:

Basis	$106,500
Improvement	25,000
Adjusted basis	$131,500

Tip

Anything that raises the basis will usually reduce your taxes. Anything that lower the basis will usually increase your taxes. Remember that the gain realized is determined by subtracting adjusted basis from adjusted sales price. The closer (higher) the basis is to the sales price, the less the gain realized. The further (lower) the basis is from the sales price, the greater the gain realized.

Let's consider three examples in determining the gain realized from the sale. In the first, there was no change in the basis. In the next two, the basis was adjusted as described above:

1. No change in basis

Net sales price	$137,500
Adjusted Basis	−106,500
Gain realized	$ 31,000

2. Basis adjusted downward

Net sales price	$137,500
Adjusted basis	−91,500
Gain realized	$ 46,000

3. Basis adjusted upward

Net sales price	$137,500
Adjusted basis	−131,500
Gain realized	$ 6,000

Gain Realized

The gain realized from the sale of the property, thus, is determined by the difference between the net sales price and the adjusted basis. Keep in mind, however, that the gain recognized (added to taxable income) may be different. For example, if the house is a personal residence and meets the rules for deferral (discussed in the previous chapter as well as in Chapter 4), none of the gain realized may be recognized in the year of sale. (Also, fix-up costs may be expensed as noted above.)

Trap

There is a tendency to confuse "equity" with "gain." It's important to maintain the distinction. Many people mistakenly consider what they have "in" their property to be equal to their gain. In fact, the gain may be substantially different (more or less) than the equity.

Gain versus Equity

Let's say that you owned property which you depreciated for 15 years to the tune of $45,000. When you sell, that $45,000 will be used to lower your basis. In other words, it will raise your gain.

However, your mortgage probably did not go down by $45,000. It may still be quite high. Thus, the equity in the property (the difference between net sales price and mortgage balance) could be significantly less than the gain realized.

Calculating Gain		
Adjusted sales price		$137,500
Basis	$100,000	
Depreciation	−45,000	
Adjusted basis	$ 55,000	−55,000
Gain realized		$ 82,500
Calculating "Equity"		
Sales price after expenses		$140,000
Loan payoff		−90,000
Net cash from sale		$ 50,000

In the above example, your equity is only $50,000 received as cash from the sale. Yet, your gain realized would be $82,500. If the $82,500 is recognized as gain, you will end up adding it to your taxable income. In other words, most of your "equity" will vanish, used up to pay taxes on the sale.

Trap

This effect may be further exacerbated if you refinanced during the term of ownership and took some of your equity out in cash. This would raise your mortgage amount, and, upon sale, you could conceivably be in a position where you didn't get in enough cash to pay the taxes you owed.

Tip

This is the reason why so many properties that are not personal residences are traded these days. The trade usually keeps the gain realized from being recognized (it is deferred or rolled over into the new property). Trades are explained in Chapter 10.

3

Deductions Available on Personal Residences

When you buy a home in which to live, you immediately acquire tax deductions. Although Congress has limited some of these deductions and there are signs these limitations may be increased in the future, as of this writing these deductions are quite significant. In this chapter we will examine them in detail.

Property Taxes

As of this writing, all property taxes that you pay on your principal residence as well as on any other residences are fully deductible. These include taxes paid on both your real property (real estate) and personal property that is part of the home and whose value is included in the assessment from which your property tax bill is prepared.

Trap

However, special assessments for local benefits, such as sidewalks and street lighting that are made against property benefited, are not deductible. The theory is that these assessments are essentially payment for improvements and betterments to your house, rather than recurrent services.

Tip

An exception applies, however, for the portion of a special assessment that relates to, and is identified as being more, either interest (on bonds sold to finance the improvements) or maintenance: These are not considered benefits, so the tax is deductible.

Tip

Your principal residence is your main home or the place where you live the majority of the time. It may be a single family house, a condo, a co-op, a mobile home, or even a houseboat.

To get the deduction for property taxes, however, you must itemize your deductions when you fill out your federal income taxes. The deduction for property taxes is taken on the "Itemized Deductions" page, Schedule A.

Interest

You may also deduct interest, subject to certain limitations, that you pay on the mortgage on your personal residence. But, you may only deduct interest in the year that it is due. You cannot deduct "prepaid" interest.

In years past taxpayers would pay interest on mortgages years in advance and then deduct that interest in 1 year, giving them a very large deduction. They did this to offset a particularly large income in that year. This practice was prohibited about 20 years ago. Today, prepaid interest may not be deducted except over the period to which it relates.

Tip

You can get a one-time increase in your interest deduction by paying 13 months worth of mortgage payments in a single year. It works like this:

Normally, you would make 12 monthly mortgage payments. However, unlike rent, mortgage interest is not due until the end of the month. For example, when you make your January mortgage payment, you are actually paying for the interest charged during the previous December.

However, if you make your January mortgage payment on December 31, you can include it in the previous year's payments; you are only paying interest that has already accrued. (Remember, the payment due January 1 is for December's interest.) Thus in 1 year you can make 13 payments, giving you an added deduction that year.

Trap

This only works for 1 year. The next year, you again have to make a payment on December 31 in order to just get 12 payments in. If you wait until the turn of the year, you would only get in 11 payments. You must continue making the "early" payment in order to maintain 12 monthly payments.

Further, your mortgage company very likely will not show the extra payment on the interest paid year-end statement it sends to you and forwards to the government. Therefore, you will need to make a special note reconciling the difference between the larger interest deduction you take and the smaller interest deduction reported by the mortgage company.

Some taxpayers send in their January payment early, say the middle of December, so that it is included in the mortgage company's statement of interest paid during the previous year.

Interest Deduction on Your Home

You can generally deduct the interest you pay on a loan on your principal residence or a second (vacation) home, subject to certain limitations. The loan can be in the form of a mortgage, deed of trust, home equity loan, line of credit, or first, second, or higher mortgage.

The limitations on your ability to deduct all of the mortgage interest you pay have to do with three criteria:

1. The size of the mortgage
2. What you did with the money you borrowed
3. When you borrowed it

Mortgages Before October 13, 1987

The interest on any and all mortgages that you took out which were secured by your principal residence or your second home prior to the above date is fully deductible. There are no limitations. This interest is called "grandfathered" since it occurred before the limitation law took effect.

Trap

You must have completed financing on the property with the loan in place by the October 13, 1987, deadline. If the house was in escrow, but the loan was not approved and the deed not transferred until after this date, other rules apply.

Tip

Generally speaking, if you don't have other home interest payments that you are making, all the interest on mortgages totaling up to a million dollars is deductible. However, as of this writing, some members of Congress have been speaking of reducing the overall amount of the mortgages to $300,000 or less. It's something to keep in mind.

Mortgages After October 13, 1987

If you borrowed money on your principal residence after the above date, separate rules apply. These have to do with your purpose in securing the money. If you took out a loan to:

Build a home

Buy a home

Improve your home

the interest on the loan up to a maximum of one million dollars is deductible. However, the amount is reduced by any interest that is deductible under the "grandfather" rule above. (If you are married and filing a separate return, the maximum amount is $500,000.)

Trap

If you had over a million dollars in mortgages prior to October 13, 1987, no mortgage interest on new loans taken out after that date can be deducted, at least until the old loan is paid off. Remember, interest on mortgages taken out after October 13, 1987, is limited to a million dollars of mortgage value, reduced *by any grandfathered interest.*

If you took out a mortgage after October 13, 1987, for any purpose other than to buy, build, or improve your home, the amount of the mortgage on which interest can be deducted is limited to $100,000. (If you are married and file a separate return, the amount is $50,000.)

Trap

It may seem obvious, but it's important to remember that limitations refer to the loaned amount, not the interest paid. The limit noted above is for a mortgage amount of not more than $100,000. It does not refer to interest of $100,000.

In short, as the tax code currently reads, you can now borrow up to a million dollars ($500,000 filing separately) to buy, build, or improve your home, and the interest on the money will be deductible. If, however, you use the proceeds for anything else, including college tuition for your kids or a vacation, the limits are $100,000 if married ($50,000 filing separately).

Tip

Interest on loans not secured by your home, such as credit card interest, is no longer deductible. Therefore, many people have chosen a home equity loan when they want long-term credit, rather than the more traditional credit card. These home equity loans can often be arranged as a "revolving" credit plan and so work just the same, for practical purposes, as a credit card.

Trap

Be aware that taking out a home equity loan reduces your equity in your property. Further, as we'll see shortly, while your equity is reduced, the tax base on which your capital gain is figured when you sell, does not change. This means that if you borrow heavily, then sell, you may end up with a small amount of cash coming out of the property and a large tax bill.

How Deductible Is Your Home Interest?

Interest on mortages taken out prior to October 13, 1987	Fully deductible
Interest on mortgages taken out after October 13, 1987, used to buy, build, or improve your home including any "grandfathered" from above	$1 Million deductible ($500,000 separate return)
Interest on mortgages taken out after October 13, 1987, used for any other purpose	$100,000 deductible ($50,000 separate return)

Special Circumstances

Refinancing Grandfathered Debt

If you refinance any debt which you originally incurred on your home prior to October 13, 1987, the interest is deductible up to the amount of the principal remaining on the mortgage. Any amount over the remaining principal is treated according to the rules for debt incurred after October 13, 1987.

Purchase of Tax-Free Income

You cannot deduct the interest on your home mortgage taken out after October 13, 1987, if you use the money to buy stocks or securities that produce tax-free income.

Mixed-Use Mortgage

If you took out a mortgage and used part of the money to improve your property and part to take a vacation, the improvement part would be subject to one set of limitations and the vacation part to another set.

For example, you borrow $250,000 on your home. You use $130,000 to improve the property and use the other $120,000 to go on a round-the-world vacation as well as buy a car. The interest on the $130,000 used for improvements is deductible, assuming you haven't exceeded the $1 million limitation. However, only the interest—$100,000—of the $120,000 used for vacation and car is deductible.

Trap

If you had a home equity line of credit in place on October 13, 1987, the interest on the amount borrowed as of that date was "grandfathered" and fully deductible. However, any amounts borrowed on the home equity line of credit after that date are subject to the "mixed mortgage" rules discussed above.

Vacation Home

If you have a second home, the limitations described above apply to a combination of both homes. You do not get separate limitations on each. If you own more than two homes, you cannot deduct additional amounts of interest. The interest on only a maximum of two homes may be deducted.

Casualty Losses

A casualty loss means that your home or a portion of it was damaged or destroyed through an accident or an act of nature. When this happens, you may be able to deduct a portion of your loss on your income taxes. However, strict limitations and rules apply. Losses which could be considered casualty may be caused by:

Earthquake and volcanic activity

Fire

Flood

Conditions of weather such as storms, tornadoes, hurricanes, drought, etc.

Vandalism

Sonic booms

The idea here is that something happens to your property which damages or destroys all or part of it in a short period of time. If that's the case, you can deduct a portion of the loss you incurred, subject to limitations.

On the other hand, losses attributable to natural deterioration and other conditions that take a long time to operate are not considered to result from casualties. Termite damage and dry rot are common examples of nondeductible losses, even if the problem is only noticed when something dramatic happens (like a wall collapsing).

Casualty Loss Limitations

Generally speaking, you must declare a casualty loss and take the deduction in the year in which it occurs. This applies even if you wait and make replacements or repairs in later years.

Tip

If you get compensation for living expenses (because your house was damaged by fire, as an example), it is not considered compensation, and you do not need to deduct it from your casualty loss.

Trap

If you are compensated for living expenses, you will need to report the amount of compensation up to your normal monthly housing expenses as regular income. If there is an additional compensation (for example, the insurance company pays you more than your monthly housing expense because it costs more to rent a motel than to stay in your home), you do not need to report that amount as income.

The following are casualty loss limitations:

1. *Nonbusiness property.* These rules apply only if the loss happened to your home or vacation home. Separate rules apply if it was a rental or business property.

2. *Reduce loss by insurance compensation.* The first thing you must do is reduce any loss you incur by any insurance payment you receive. For example, if your house burns down and your loss is $50,000, but the insurance company picks up the entire tab, you have no deductible casualty loss for tax purposes.

3. Next, you must deduct $100 from the loss. The $100 applies to each loss but only once if many properties are involved.

4. Finally, you must reduce your total loss by 10 percent of your gross adjusted income. In other words, if you have a loss of $50,000 and your insurance company does not compensate you in any way, you would first reduce it by $100 and then by 10 percent of your gross adjusted income. If your adjusted gross income (AGI) was $60,000, the following would apply:

Total loss	$50,000
Less $100	–49,900
Less 10% of AGI	–6,000
Casualty loss	$43,900

Tip

Losses for both casualty and theft can be combined so that the 10 percent of adjusted gross income rule only applies once. See your accountant for the specific calculation.

Trap

Both the $100 limitation and the 10 percent reduction apply to each person (married people are considered one person for this purpose) who suffers a loss from the same event. For example, you and your wife own a home with your brother and sister. You and your wife will have the $100 limitation and the 10 percent reduction applied to your loss. Your brother and sister will each have the $100 and 10 percent applied to them as well.

Calculating Your Loss

The amount you can deduct for a loss depends to a large extent on the amount you originally paid for your property. For a home, it is the *lesser* of the adjusted basis of the property or its loss in fair market value.

For a home or other nonbusiness property, all of the property including plants, trees, buildings, garages, pools, decks, etc., are figured together when calculating the loss.

For example, you have a home with an adjusted basis of $110,000. (You originally paid $90,000 and added a room which cost $20,000.) There was an earthquake which damaged the home and it required extensive repairs. The cost of the repairs totaled $60,000.

You had an appraisal done which established the fair market value both before and after the earthquake. Before, the house was worth $200,000. After, it was worth $160,000. The following calculations can be made:

Adjusted basis	$110,000
Fair market value before	200,000
Fair market value after	−160,000
Loss in fair market value	$ 40,000

Since the loss in fair market value is lower than the adjusted basis, that is your casualty loss; in this case it is $40,000. Note that we are here calculating only the loss of real property. If you have a personal property loss such as furniture, car, clothing, etc., that were part of the overall loss, you must determine the amount of loss separately for each item of personal property. However, you then combine the personal and real property losses for purposes of using the $100 limit and the 10 percent of gross adjusted income reduction.

Tip

The actual cost of repairs may be more (as in this case) or less than the casualty loss. The repair costs, while they should be taken into account by the appraiser, do not determine the casualty loss. Rather, it is the lesser of the decrease in fair market value or the adjusted basis of the property.

Trap

Your cost in hiring an appraiser as well as other costs such as an accountant's fees in determining your casualty loss are assumed to be expenses involved in determining how much tax you must pay. Hence, they may not be added to your casualty loss. (You may be able to deduct them, however, as a miscellaneous deduction on your itemized deductions, subject, of course, to the 2 percent of adjusted gross income limit but probably not if the property was your principal residence.)

Decline in Market Value

A decline in market value that is not directly due to the casualty is not deductible. For example, Smith's home is damaged in an earthquake and the damage costs $20,000 to repair. However, because people are now afraid to move into that area, the loss in value is $100,000. Smith's deductible loss will be initially determined by the $20,000 repair cost, less insurance and the "tax haircuts" discussed above.

Casualty Gain

It is possible that you could have a casualty gain. This might occur if the insurance company paid you more than the basis of your home. In that case you would need to report this as a capital gain on Schedule D of your federal income taxes or in some cases, on form 4797. (See an accountant for details of using the proper form.) However, if you reinvest the proceeds of insurance in replacement property bought within 2 years, this gain can be deferred.

Deductions on the Sale or Purchase of a Home

When you sell or purchase a home, certain deductions may be

available to you that are not offered to those with rental properties. For example, you may be eligible to "roll over" the gain you
receive (discussed in Chapter 4) or exclude up to $125,000 of the
gain provided you are 55 years old and meet certain restrictions
(discussed in Chapter 5). A number of other deductions are also
available including those discussed below.

Costs of Sale

Generally speaking you can deduct most costs of sale from the
amount you receive. This includes real estate agents' fees, closing costs, and other charges of sale.

Fixing-Up Costs

For a principal residence, you may deduct your costs of fixing up
the property for sale (subject to certain limits noted below) when
you figure the amount you realized from the sale. These may
only be deducted when figuring the gain that is rolled over into
another property.

Trap

You may *not* deduct fixing-up expenses if you simply sell your
home and do not then defer the gain by purchasing another
home. In other words, if the gain is recognized, no fixing-up
expenses may be deducted

There are certain limitations to the fixing-up expenses. Only
expenses incurred during the 90-day period prior to the date you
sign the sales contract with the buyer may be deducted. Further,
all of these expenses must be paid within 30 days after the date
the sale was concluded.

Other rules require that you do not use these expenses as deductions when calculating your taxable income; that they be for such
things as painting, decorating, and repairing and not be improvements or capital expenditures; and that you not use them as deductions when you make the calculation for gain realized on the sale.

Tip

Your fixing-up expenses are deducted from the amount you

received from the sale much as real estate commission or escrow charges are. However, any capital expenditures or improvements, such as putting in a new water heater or adding a new garage door, can be added to your tax base (discussed in Chapter 2). In this manner they will reduce the gain you receive from the sale.

Interest Deduction

When you sell or purchase a home, certain amounts of interest may be deducted. On the sale of the home, all the interest you pay on your existing mortgages (up to the limitations noted above) may be deducted from your ordinary income up to the day of the close of escrow but not including the date of close of escrow.

When you purchase a home, the interest you "prepay" as part of the closing may be deducted but only in the year it is due. For example, you purchase a home on December 15, 1992. The lender requires that you prepay 16 days of interest, until December 31, as a requirement for getting the mortgage. Your first payment, however, is not due until February 1, 1993. (Remember, you pay in arrears on a mortgage. The interest for January, in this case, isn't due until the first of February.)

The interest on your mortgage prepaid during escrow would be deductible in 1992. The interest paid beginning on February 1 would be deductible in 1993.

Points

You may also be able to deduct some of the points that you pay when you purchase your home in the year you paid them. However, the rules for deduction of points are quite strict and many home owners find that they actually cannot deduct all or any of them.

Note: The following rules on deduction of points apply only to your principal residence. They do not apply to a vacation or second home or to rental property.

Generally speaking, in order to be able to deduct in the same year the points that you pay on a mortgage, you must meet the following requirements:

1. The loan must be to improve or purchase your principal residence. If it's a refinance and you use part to improve and part for other purposes, only the points representing the part used to improve the property may be deducted.

2. The points to secure a loan must be an "established business practice" in your area. In other words, if you're in an area where points are not normally charged (it's hard to conceive of such an area existing), you wouldn't be able to deduct the points.

3. The points you paid must not exceed the amount generally charged. For example, if all the other lenders are charging two points for a given interest rate and you go to a lender who is charging five points, you probably will only be able to deduct a maximum of two points in the year of purchase. The remaining three points can, however, be deducted over the lifespan of the mortgage.

4. The points must be computed as a *percentage* of the principal amount of the loan. In other words, they cannot be a set fee. They must be 1 percent, 2 percent, or some other similar amount calculated on the amount you borrowed.

5. You must not pay for the points out of the amount borrowed. If you're getting a home improvement loan, you must pay for the points out of additional funds. If you're buying, you must provide for the points out of your own pocket, not out of the mortgage.

Tip

When purchasing a property, it is sometimes difficult to separate which funds are contributed by the buyer and which come from the mortgage. Therefore, many buyers in the past have paid into escrow a separate check which specifically states it is to go for the mortgage points. A better plan is to have the charges itemized on the closing statement specifically showing where the money you paid went.

Trap

If you are a seller and as part of the sales agreement you pay some of the buyer's points, you cannot deduct these points as interest from your taxes. You can, however, consider them as an expenses of selling and use them to reduce your adjusted sales price.

Other Costs at Time of Purchase

Only points, as described above, may be deducted in the year paid as interest. Everything else is considered a fee, including recording and document costs, appraisals and credit reports, etc.

Improvements

Any improvements that you make to your property during the time you own it may be added to the tax base. As noted earlier, increasing your tax base ultimately will result in lowering the gain you receive from the sale of the property. (Remember, the gain is the difference between the adjusted sales price or what you got from the sale and the tax base. If you raise the tax base, and you automatically reduce the gain on which taxes may be due).

Tip

Savvy home owner save all of their receipts for home improvements and capital expenditures. Doing this means that at the time of sale, you can add these to your tax base. Receipts for items which you purchase for your home and which you want to save may include the following:

Room additions

Plumbing repairs such as adding a new water heater or replacing kitchen cabinets and tile

Landscaping

Adding blinds which go with the house

Adding new light fixtures

Adding a pool

Note: Painting and redecorating generally are not considered a capital expenditure. However, adding new carpeting may be considered so.

**Items Which May Not Be Used to
Adjust the Basis of Your Home**

As noted, the basis of your property may be raised or lowered depending on the item. However, for a principal residence, the following may *not* be used to raise or lower basis:

Nondeductible points as defined earlier

Cost of repairs

FHA mortgage insurance premium

Utility charges

Items deducted as moving expenses

Fire insurance premium

Conversion to a Rental

Different tax rules apply to homes which are your personal residence and houses which you rent out. Therefore, if you convert your home to a rental or vice versa, you must take care to be sure that you understand these rules and that you don't move from a tax advantageous situation to a tax disadvantageous one. In this section we are going to look at some of the basic considerations with regard to conversion. However, you may also want to look at Chapter 7 for further information on part personal and part rental use of a vacation home.

Reasons for Converting

There are many reasons that you may want to convert a home to a rental. You may have bought another home and have decided that your present one would make a good investment. So, you now plan to rent it out over an extended period of time.

Or you may have a temporary change in employment that requires you to reside elsewhere. During the period of time that you are away, you may want to rent out your home. Or you may want to rent out a portion of your home to gain extra income. Or you may purchase and move into a new home with the intention of selling your old one. But market conditions may prevent such a sale, so instead you rent out the property.

Possible Consequences of Converting

Two of the biggest advantages of selling a personal residence, as opposed to selling a rental, are that you may be able to defer your capital gain into the new property (discussed in Chapter 4) and you may be able to claim a once-in-a-lifetime exclusion of gain up to $125,000 (discussed in Chapter 5). However, if you convert your home into a permanent rental, you lose both of these advantages. Rental property does not qualify for the deferral of gain or for the once-in-a-lifetime exclusion.

Trap

Many people confuse "residential" property with "personal residence." Residential property refers to any home in which people live, as opposed to commercial or industrial property. A personal residence is the one home in which you reside. Your personal residence may qualify for the rollover and for the once-in-a-lifetime exclusion. But, just because a property is residential does not mean it will qualify. Residential rental property, as noted earlier, does not qualify. Thus, when you convert your principal residence to a rental, you take the chance of losing tax advantages.

Advantages of Conversion

Although rental property does not allow for deferral of gain on sale (except through a trade) or the $125,000 exclusion, it does have other advantages. For example, as noted in Chapter 6, you may deduct virtually all of your costs as expenses for rental property. In addition, you may also be able to depreciate property, thus reducing income. Typical deductions for rental property include the following:

Taxes

Mortgage interest

Insurance

Maintenance

Repairs

Depreciation

What this means is that your total expenses, particularly when depreciation is added in, may amount to more than your total rental income, thus producing a loss.

Trap

The 1986 Tax Reform Act considers real estate a category of "passive" activity. Essentially this means that you cannot deduct real estate losses from your ordinary income, such as wages, salaries, interest, and dividends.

Tip

There is an exception to the above rule and it states that if your income is below $100,000 a year, you may deduct up to $25,000 in passive real estate losses from it. As your income increases above $100,000, you lose 50 cents of deduction for each dollar of income until at $150,000 of income, no passive real estate losses may be deducted. This is explained in detail in Chapter 5.

Temporary Conversion

Most of the problems revolving around converting a home to a rental arise when the conversion is temporary. How do you treat the property while it is a rental? Later on can you convert back to a personal residence and get the rollover and exclusion advantages? Unfortunately, the rules here tend to be in a gray area. You should check with your accountant or tax advisor for the latest thinking on the matter. Here are some general guidelines which may apply as of this writing:

Intention.   If your intention is to create a rental property, then, generally speaking, you may claim all of the expenses as noted earlier including a tax loss subject, of course, to the passive activity rules. However, depreciation will be based on the lower of the property's original cost and its fair market value at the time of conversion.

If you later change your mind and decide to claim the property as a personal residence, sell it, and then want the rollover and exclusion benefits, you may still be able to get these provided:

1. You move back into the property and reestablish it as your principal residence. While there is no hard-and-fast rule for how long you must occupy the property for this purpose, it is generally accepted that moving back in for a minimum of 6 months is probably required.

2. You claim that you never abandoned the property as your personal residence. Rather, you only rented it out temporarily. There are, however, problems with doing this. One of them is time. If you haven't lived in the property for an extended period of time, it may be difficult for you to claim the home as your principal residence.

Tip

There is no set maximum amount of time beyond which you can no longer claim the property as your principal residence without moving back in. However, some tax advisors have suggested that 2 years is a likely maximum period. This corresponds to the 2-year time limit that you have to find a replacement property when you sell your home. Be advised, however, that there is no set rule here. Check with your own tax advisor.

Trap

The IRS in the past has denied deductions on homes converted to rentals when the intent was to convert them only temporarily. For example, you bought a new home and temporarily rented out your old one while waiting for it to sell. The IRS has held that in this situation your intent was not to convert to a rental and that you could only deduct your rental expenses to the extent of your rental income. You could not, in other words, deduct or carry forward losses in excess of income.

The Ninth Circuit Court of Appeals, however, has overturned the IRS position [Bolaris v. Commissioner, 776 F.2d 1328 (1985)].

When Converted.   If you convert your property from home use to rental use at the beginning of the year, you can treat the property as a rental for the entire year for the purposes of deducting depreciation and other expenses. However, if you convert during the year, you must divide the year into that portion used for rental and that portion for personal use.

Only a Portion Converted. If you convert only a portion of your home, say a bedroom, to a rental, only that portion may be treated as rental property. The remainder will be considered your home. Consult your tax advisor about how to handle this in your specific case.

Converted Vacation Property. As noted earlier when you convert a vacation home to a rental, then to a home, then to part vacation/rental property, special rules apply. See Chapter 7 for an explanation of how vacation property is handled.

Expenses While Offered for Sale. If you vacate your home and list it with a real estate agent, you cannot treat it as a rental property. You cannot deduct rental expenses such as depreciation.

Losses upon Sale. If you convert a personal residence to rental use and later sell it at a loss, you are allowed to deduct some of the loss from income, as you can with "pure" rental property. However, you must consider as your basis only the fair market value of the property at the time of conversion, if it is lower than your actual cost. The IRS will not allow you a deduction for a loss that economically accrued while you were using the property for personal or residential purposes, even if you realize it after conversion.

Moreover, if you just vacate the house, list it for sale, and because it is a down market, you actually sell the house for less than its fair value when you moved out, you probably get no deduction for the loss. You have not "actually converted" it to income-producing uses, according to the IRS and most courts.

These, then, are the various deductions that you may claim either from your ordinary income in the year the expense occurred or upon sale of the property when you own a personal residence.

4

Sale of Personal Residence

Every year approximately 3½ million home owners sell their personal residence. The vast majority of these people sell their property for a higher price, sometimes significantly higher, than the amount for which they purchased it. (Because most home owners have held their property for a long period of time, even during the recent housing recession, sales were usually for more than original purchase prices.) As a result, there is often a tax to consider upon sale.

Realized Gain

If you sell your residence for a profit, taking into account the net selling price (after commissions and other expenses of sale) and your adjusted "basis" (taking into account improvements that you made, any depreciation that you were able to take because of business or rental use, and other required adjustments), you have a "realized gain." (If you're not sure about how to calculate basis and gain, recheck Chapter 2.)

The general rule is that all realized gains are taxable. However, the tax law provides for two important exceptions to this rule, which if applicable to your situation, could save or defer many thousands of dollars of tax liability.

Tip

Don't make the assumption that just because you sold your house, you must pay taxes on your gain in the year of sale. You have to live somewhere and as long as you purchase a new home, observing the guidelines that follow, you may be able to defer paying taxes on the gain you realized almost indefinitely.

The first exception is the "rollover" rule for gains on the sale of principal residence. Any taxpayer can take advantage of this exception, generally for as many profitable sales as he or she makes. The second advantage is the $125,000 exclusion, which is applicable only to one sale in a lifetime and is available only to taxpayers who have reached the age of 55 years.

Trap

Keep in mind that if neither of these exceptions apply (as explained below), the gain on sale of your residence is normally treated as a long-term capital gain, which will be subject to a maximum tax rate of 28 percent under current law.

Rollover Rule—General Requirements

Gain on the sale of a principal residence is "recognized"—meaning subject to current tax—according to the following rules:

1. It is taxable only to the extent that the "net sales price," less qualified fixing-up expenses, exceeds the purchase price of a *replacement* principal residence.
2. That replacement principal residence must be acquired by the taxpayer within a 4-year period.
3. That 4-year period begins 2 years before the date of sale of the old residence and ends 2 years after that date.

Any gain that is not recognized according to this rule is deferred.

Tip

In calculating the new basis, you reduce the basis on the replacement residence by the amount of the gain that is not recognized on the old residence.

Trap

Contrary to some popular opinion, the rollover rule is not "elective." You can't choose to defer. Rather, if you qualify under the rule, you must defer. The gain cannot be recognized if the legal requirements for nonrecognition are met.

Deferral Example 1

Tom's adjusted basis in his old residence is $200,000. He sells the residence in 1993 for an adjusted sales price of $320,000, thereby realizing a $120,000 gain. However, in 1994, he buys a new residence for $350,000. Tom's $120,000 gain is not recognized at all because the purchase price of the new residence exceeds the adjusted selling price of the old residence. His initial basis for the new residence is $230,000—the $350,000 purchase price less $120,000 of unrecognized gain.

Gain on old residence	
Net sales price	$320,000
Adjusted basis	−200,000
Realized gain	$120,000

Treatment of new residence	
Purchase price	$350,000
Reduced by unrecognized gain of old residence	−120,000
Initial basis of new residence	$230,000

Tip

Remember, if the replacement residence cost does not exceed the sales price of the old residence, you may still be able to roll over a portion, though not all, of the gain.

Deferral Example 2

The facts are the same as in example 1, except that the purchase price of the new residence is only $300,000. Because Tom's purchase price is $20,000 less than the adjusted selling price of the old residence, $20,000 of the $120,000 gain realized is recognized, and only $100,000 is not recognized. Tom must pay tax, as a capital gain, on the $20,000 recognized gain.

His adjusted basis in the new residence is $200,000; that is, the purchase price of $300,000, less the $100,000 of gain that was not recognized. Notice that in this case, the adjusted basis of the new residence is the same as the adjusted basis of the old residence at the time of its sale.

Gain on old residence	
Net sales price	$320,000
Adjusted basis	−200,000
Realized gain	$120,000

Treatment of new residence	
Purchase price	$300,000
Reduced by portion of realized gain of old residence	−100,000
Initial basis of new residence	$200,000

Gain recognized (taxed in current year)	
Realized gain	$120,000
Deferred portion of gain	−100,000
Portion of realized gain on old residence that is recognized (taxed in current year)	$ 20,000

Tip

Remember, you have a 4-year window in which to replace the property sold. You do not have to buy the replacement property only "after" the sale of your old residence. It can actually be purchased up to 2 years "before" the sale.

Deferral Example 3

The facts are the same as in example 1, except that the purchase price of the new residence is only $180,000. The adjusted basis for the new residence will be its purchase price, $180,000. All of Tom's realized gain was recognized, so no adjustment to the actual purchase price of the new residence is necessary to determine tax basis.

Gain on old residence	
Net sales price	$320,000
Adjusted basis	−200,000
Realized gain	$120,000

Treatment of new residence	
Purchase price and initial basis of new residence	$180,000

Gain recognized (taxed in current year)	
Realized gain	$120,000
Deferred portion of gain	0
Portion of realized gain on old residence that is recognized (taxed in current year)	$120,000

Tip

Note that although the selling price exceeds the amount reinvested in a new residence by $140,000 ($320,000 less $180,000), the gain recognized is only $120,000 since the gain recognized cannot exceed the gain realized.

Qualification Requirements

The rollover rule applies only when both the old property and the new property qualify as the taxpayer's "principal residence."

Principle Residence

A principal residence is your main residence, where you spend most of your time. You can only have one principal residence at a time. It can be a house, condominium, stock in a cooperative housing corporation, mobile home, or even a houseboat.

Because Congress and the IRS realize that people sometimes have to vacate their old homes and move into a new home that they have bought before they can sell the old home, the qualifications for a "principal residence" have a rather flexible interpretation. It is not necessary in this situation, for example, that the taxpayer actually *live* in the old residence up to the moment that his or her sale escrow closes.

It is even possible to rent out the old residence for a period of time after vacating it and before selling it and still not lose the benefits of rollover treatment. There is no fixed rule about how long a property can still be regarded as a principal residence after the owner physically vacates it. The IRS regulations on this point say merely that this issue is determined based:

> ...upon all the facts and circumstances in each case, including the good faith of the taxpayer. The mere fact that property is, or has been, rented is not determinative that such property is not used by the taxpayer as his principal residence. For example, if the taxpayer purchases his new residence before he sells his old residence, the fact that he temporarily rents out the new residence during the period before he vacates the old residence may not, in the light of all the facts and circumstances in the case, prevent the new residence from being considered as property used by the taxpayer as his principal residence.

One Spouse Ownership

Gain is deferrable even though, for example, the old residence was owned by only one of the spouses, while the other is bought in both their names, or *vice versa*. In fact, it is even deferrable if one spouse owned the old residence in his or her sole name, while the new residence is bought in the other's sole name.

Vacating the Old Residence or Delayed Move-In

Generally, if it is necessary to vacate the old residence, or defer moving into the new residence, for a significant period of time (over 3 months), good tax planning requires that the taxpayer make and document his or her efforts to minimize these periods.

It would not be a good idea, for example, to enter into a long-term lease of either property; month-to-month arrangements are much preferable. Also, if there are special circumstances that defer either moving out or moving in, such as construction delays, labor disputes, or medical problems, taxpayers should seek to obtain, and retain, written evidence of the problem just in case the IRS auditor should later call.

Which Is Your Principal Residence?

Sometimes there is no question that a taxpayer has been using property as a residence, but the issue is whether it is his or her (or their) principal residence. This question often arises when people own multiple properties that are used some of the time for residential purposes.

For example, suppose that a couple owns a home in suburban New York and also has a weekend cottage in the Berkshire Mountains that they have generally used during the summer and winter seasons. Most likely, the home in New York would be considered their principal residence.

But suppose now that after they retire, they move into the former weekend retreat and live in it continuously for a period of 6 months. Have they changed their "principal residence" so that only the sale of the cottage, rather than the home, will qualify for rollover? There is, unfortunately, no definite answer to this question.

Tip
_____

When two houses are involved or this is a marital dissolution, creative planning in this area can often be desirable. It may be possible to create a fact pattern for which the desired tax result is justifiable, if not absolutely certain to be achieved.

For example, a couple which has owned two separate residences and is planning to sell both of them might arrange to transfer the title of one property to the husband and the other to the wife. One of the parties might then move to the second residence for a period of several months, and occupy it for more than half of the time, while the other party continues to spend most of his or her time in the first residence. In this situation, both parties have a good-faith claim that he or she is occupying one of the residences as his or her principal residence, and if both residences are sold and either one new residence is bought in both names or two new residences are purchased, it is quite reasonable to argue that the gains on both properties can be deferred if the respective costs exceed the respective selling prices. This technique is especially important when the spouses are in the process of a marital dissolution.

Building a New Residence

Taxpayers can defer sales on old residences through building, as well as buying, new residences. However, only the cost of construction incurred within the relevant 4-year period is counted as qualified purchase price.

Example of Construction

In 1989, Tom and Nancy bought a lot for $50,000 to be used as a future home site. In 1992, they sold their principal residence for $250,000, realizing a gain of $100,000. In 1992, they began construction of a new residence on their site and incurred construction costs of $225,000. They moved into the new residence within 2 years after selling the old one. Of their realized gain of $100,000, $75,000 is not recognized. The construction costs of $225,000, but not the land cost of $50,000, count as replacement property costs. The basis for the new property will be $200,000, the purchase price of the lot plus the construction costs less the $75,000 gain that is not recognized on the sale of their old home:

Sales price of old residence	$250,000
Construction cost of new residence	−225,000
Gain recognized	$ 25,000
Gain on sale of old residence	$100,000
Gain recognized	−25,000
Gain rolled over (deferred)	$ 75,000
Purchase price of lot	$ 50,000
Construction costs	+225,000
Gain rolled over	−75,000
Basis of new property	$200,000

Partial Use of Property as Residence

If only a portion of a parcel has been used as the taxpayer's principal residence, the taxpayer must allocate his or her gain between the portion deferred and the portion not deferred, on a reasonable basis. The regulations do not indicate, however, just what methods are (or are not) reasonable.

Multiple-Unit Dwelling

If the property is a multiple-unit dwelling of which the taxpayer occupies one unit as his or her residence, it would appear proper to allocate the sales price, and the basis, on either actual respective areas occupied or relative rental values.

Multiple-Dwelling Example. Sally owns a "duplex" unit, which has an adjusted basis of $180,000. Until sale, she has occupied the ground floor apartment as her principal residence and rented out the second floor apartment. Both units are the same size. In this situation, Sally may treat 50 percent of the selling price and gain as subject to the rollover.

Tip

In the previous example, if Sally can establish that ground floor apartments are in fact more desirable than second floor units, a larger allocation to the deferrable portion may well be justified.

Home Office

If the taxpayer is able to deduct the costs of maintaining part of his or her residence because it is used as a "home office," the portion so used is likewise ineligible for rollover. However, in its most recent ruling, the IRS said that this rule applies only if the home office costs are deductible in the year in which the sale occurred.

Tip

Prior use which terminated before the year of sale is apparently not a problem. Of course, recent case law and rulings have made deductibility of costs attributable to a home office much less likely to be allowed than in the past. Check with your accountant or tax advisor for new rules regarding home office deductions.

Qualified Fixing-Up Expenses

Sometimes, the amount that must be reinvested in order to defer gain entirely can be less than the selling price of the old residence. This may occur when there are significant qualified fixing-up expenses.

The selling price of the old residence is reduced, for purposes of the rollover calculation but not for other purposes, by "qualified fixing-up expenses" incurred during the fix-up period. The rules are as follows:

1. This period starts 90 days before the taxpayer signs a contract to sell the old residence.

2. Expenses must be paid no later than 30 days after the date that the old residence is sold.

3. Expenses that are taken into account are those which are for work performed on the old residence in order to assist in its sale but which cannot otherwise be deducted or capitalized so as to increase basis. Painting and minor repairs are the most common examples of these expenses.

Example of Qualified Fixing-Up Expenses

Nancy has an adjusted basis of $150,000 in her old residence. She sells the property for a net selling price of $275,000, after incurring $4000 in repair and painting costs. Her realized gain is $125,000. However, she only needs to spend $271,000, rather than $275,000, in order to defer all of her gain. If she does, her basis in the new residence will be $125,000 less than its actual purchase price because all of her realized gain is deferred.

Net sales price of old property	$275,000
Adjusted basis	−150,000
Realized gain	$125,000
Net sales price of old property	$275,000
Less fixing-up costs	−4,000
Minimum price to be paid for new property to roll over entire realized gain	$271,000
Purchase price of new property	$271,000
Less realized gain rolled over	−125,000
Initial basis of new property	$146,000

Tip

As noted in an earlier chapter, the amount of gain realized and recognized depends on the total selling price and total purchase price of the old and new residences, respectively, not the sellers' equity in the property.

Cost Not Equity Governs

The taxpayer's "equity" is not relevant to the tax determinations, even though it often is the most critical figure in how much reinvestment can occur.

For example, Don owned his old residence, which had a $220,000 adjusted basis, free and clear of debt. He sells the residence for $300,000 and buys a new residence for $360,000, of which he pays $120,000 in cash and gives a note to the seller for $240,000. Although the two transactions result in a $180,000 "net increase" in Don's available cash (selling price of $300,00 less $120,000 down payment on new residence), all of Don's gain is not recognized. The reason is that the cost of the new residence is higher than the sales price of the old.

Cost of new residence	$360,000
Sales price of old residence	$300,000

Since the new residence costs more than the old, all of the gain realized is deferred regardless of whether it is all invested in the new property.

Disadvantages

In the prior example, the rule seemed to give Don a windfall, but it sometimes disadvantages taxpayers.

For example, Murray's house also had a $220,000 adjusted basis and a $300,000 selling price, but it was subject to a loan of $175,000. Therefore, Murray only took $125,000 out of the escrow on his old house. He uses all of this cash and incurs a new loan of $75,000 to purchase a new residence, the total cost of which is $200,000. All of Murray's $80,000 realized gain is recognized—he gets no benefit from the rollover rules, even though he invested considerably more than the net cash proceeds from the old house sale. The new house has an initial tax basis equal to its actual cost, $200,000.

Sales price of old home	$300,000
Purchase price of new home	−200,000
Difference	$100,000

Sales price of old home	$300,000
Adjusted basis	−220,000
Gain realized	$ 80,000

Difference between sales price of old home and purchase price of new home	$100,000
Gain realized	80,000
Portion of gain rolled over	0

Because the new home costs $100,000 less than the old home's sales price, the $80,000 of gain realized on the sale is recognized (taxable in the current year) and the initial tax basis of the new home is $200,000.

Multiple Rollovers

One restriction that applies to most home sales under current law is that rollover treatment is available only once every 2 years. Furthermore, if the taxpayer buys more than one principal residence within a 2-year period, only the last of those residences counts as the qualifying replacement.

Multiple Rollover Example

Within a 2-year period, Harriet sells her old residence, which had an adjusted basis of $200,000, for $300,000, buys a second residence for $350,000, sells the second residence for $400,000, and buys a new residence for $430,000 (all figures being the net sales price).

Harriet's $100,000 gain on the sale of the first residence can be "rolled over" into the third house, but the gain on the sale of the second residence, $50,000, is not eligible for rollover unless the special "job-related rule" described below applies. The adjusted basis of the third house is $330,000, its cost of $430,000 less the $100,000 gain not recognized on the sale of the first house.

Gain realized on sale of first home	$100,000

Gain realized on sale of second home	50,000
Gain rolled over into third home	100,000
Gain recognized and taxable in current year (from second home)	50,000

Job-Related Sale

The once-in-2-years limitation does not apply, however, if the second sale was in connection with the commencement of work as an employee or self-employed individual at a new place of work which is quite far from the location of the second home owned.

Tip

In order to qualify, the distance from the taxpayer's second home location to the new place of work must be at least 35 miles more than the distance from the third home to the new place of work. Moreover, the taxpayer must remain in the new principal place of work for at least 39 weeks in the year following his or her arrival if he or she commences work as an employee and at least 78 weeks during the 2-year period following his or her arrival if he or she commences work as a self-employed individual.

Job-Related Sale Example

In the prior example, assume that Harriet sold her second home and bought her third home because she changed jobs from a location in Los Angeles to a new location in Phoenix, Arizona. The gain on the second home, as well as the gain on the first home, qualifies for nonrecognition. Therefore, Harriet is not subject to tax on either gain, and her adjusted basis in the third home will be $280,000—the $430,000 cost less total gain not recognized of $150,000.

Gain realized on sale of first home	$100,000
Gain realized on sale of second home	50,000
Gain rolled over into third home	150,000
Gain recognized and taxable in current year (from second home)	0

Tip

As this chapter is written, a tax reform bill is pending in Congress which would, if enacted in its current form, repeal the 2-year limitation on rollover treatment and treat all sales of homes under the rules that presently apply to job-related sales of homes. It was not, however, included in the tax bill passed in August 1993.

Tax Reporting of Rollover Gains

Anyone who sells a principal residence at a gain must complete IRS Form 2119 and attach it to his or her federal tax return for the year of sale. This is true whether or not a qualifying replacement property has been purchased by the time the return is filed. If it is not yet bought, but the seller expects to make a qualifying rollover purchase, the seller must answer "Yes" to the applicable question on the form.

When a replacement property is actually found, an amended Form 2119 should be attached to the return for the year in which the purchase occurs. If the taxpayer ultimately does not replace the property within the 2-year qualifying period, in such a way as to defer all of the gain realized, he or she must file an amended return for the year in which the sale originally occurred and report the gain as taxable in that year.

Trap

Until the IRS is notified that replacement did not occur, the statute of limitations for assessing tax based upon the taxability of the gain will not start to run against the IRS. Therefore if you don't follow through with a new home acquisition, you may be surprised with a tax bill many years after the normal 3-year period after your return is filed, unless you provide the IRS with written notice.

5
The $125,000 Exclusion

The rollover rule discussed in the last chapter allows many Americans to defer paying taxes on the realized gain of their home by rolling that gain over into subsequent homes. These rollovers can continue on indefinitely into ever more expensive homes. Similarly, a taxpayer who simply owns a home for a long time may have seen the price double and even quadruple as real estate prices in general skyrocketed during the previous two decades. (Even recent price declines during recession have not wiped away much of the earlier price increases for many owners.) As a result of the rollover or price appreciation or of simply buying a large home, many Americans reach retirement age with a big, expensive house.

However, upon retirement, many people no longer want the burden of a high mortgage associated with a high-priced property. Also, at retirement, with their families grown and out of the house, they often want a smaller and, consequently, less expensive home.

It is here, however, that having used the rollover earlier or having lived in a home for a long time can prove disadvantageous. To sell and then buy another smaller, less expensive home may mean that a large amount of realized gain (perhaps rolled over many times) will become recognized and tax will be due on it in the current year. Attempting to sell and downsize, in short, can become a tax trap that forces retirees to pay a significant portion of what may be their biggest "grubstake," the equity in their home, to taxes. This can adversely affect retirement plans and can pressure taxpayers to continue living in larger, more expensive homes than they want upon retirement.

In order to correct this problem, the government created a special provision of the tax code which allows the taxpayer to, once in a lifetime, at age 55 or older, and upon meeting certain guidelines explained below, exclude up to $125,000 of gain recognized on the sale of a personal residence.

The effect of this rule is to allow a backdoor, a way out, for the person who is nearing retirement age and wants to downsize. It allows the taxpayer to sell and move to a less expensive personal residence without losing a very large chunk of equity to taxes.

Rules for the $125,000 Exclusion

Up to $125,000 of gain on the sale of property may be totally excluded from gross income, if all of these conditions are satisfied:

1. The property sold was owned and used by the taxpayer as his or her principal residence for at least 3 years during the 5-year period ending on the date of the sale.
2. The seller is at least 55 years old when the sale occurs.
3. The seller elects to exclude the gain from gross income.
4. Neither the seller nor his or her spouse had previously elected to exclude gain on the sale of property from gross income under this provision, other than an election made with respect to a sale that occurred on or before July 26, 1978.

Tip

It's important to understand that there is no requirement that any proceeds be reinvested in qualifying replacement property in order to take advantage of this benefit. This is not a rollover.

If you like, you can use the money to take an extended vacation or whatever.

Strict compliance with the requirements of this section (121) is necessary, and proper timing is often required to get full benefit from the exclusion.

Criteria for Use as a Principal Residence

The criteria for deciding whether property has been used as a principal residence are basically the same as those discussed in the prior chapter, where the issue was whether gain could be "rolled over" tax free. Of course, it is not necessary to determine whether the property is the taxpayer's principal residence at the time of sale, only whether it was his or her principal residence during *3 of the 5 years before the date of sale.*

Temporary Absences

The regulations say that "short temporary absences such as for vacation or other seasonal absence" are disregarded in determining whether the 3-year period of use is satisfied. However, an absence of as long as 1 year will not be disregarded, according to an example in the regulations.

Physically or Mentally Incapable

A special rule, however, may be applicable. If the taxpayer is physically or mentally incapable of self-care and has used the property during the 5 years before sale for at least 1 year as a principal residence, the seller will be treated as using the property as his or her principal residence during any part of the 5-year period that the taxpayer owned the property and resided in any facility, including a nursing home, which was licensed by the state or city to care for an individual in the taxpayer's condition.

Inherited Property

A widow or widower who inherits property from a deceased spouse may also inherit the ownership and occupancy status of the decedent. Thus, the decedent's use is attributed to the present owner (the widow or widower) for purposes of ownership and use requirements.

Inherited Property Example

Mary's husband, James, owned a home and used it as his principal residence continuously from 1982 through his death on May 5, 1992. He never made an election to exclude gain under Section 121. Mary occupied the property with him but was not an owner. His will left the home to Mary outright.

Under these circumstances, Mary may qualify for the exclusion if she is over the age of 55 years when she sells the home, provided that she sells it no later than May 5, 1994.

Trap

Note that in the above example, Mary must actually receive title to the house in order to take advantage of this rule. A sale by John's estate, rather than Mary individually, won't qualify for the exclusion, even if Mary is both the executor and the sole beneficiary of the estate.

Destruction of Property

Destruction of property in a casualty, and receipt of insurance proceeds, is considered a sale for purposes of Section 121.

Destruction of Property Example

Harry, a qualifying individual, had an adjusted basis of $100,000 in his home when it was destroyed in a hurricane. He recovered insurance proceeds of $210,000. Harry may elect to exclude his $110,000 gain from gross income.

Only Part Personal Residence

If only part of a property is used for residential purposes, an allocation of the gain realized between the qualifying portion and the nonqualifying portion must be made. The regulations don't state how this allocation should be made. However, the principles discussed in Chapter 4 should also apply to this area. Thus, relative area (square footage) and relative rental values would both seem reasonable bases for making the allocation.

Only One Spouse Has to Be 55 Years Old

If property is owned jointly by husband and wife, or held by them as tenants by the entireties or as community property in community property states, only one has to be over the age of 55 years in order to qualify for the exclusion, if they file a joint return for the year in which the sale occurs. Both, however, will thereafter be precluded from making a new election to exclude gain under Section 121.

Tax Planning for Exclusion

By proper planning in advance, it may be possible to use this exclusion when otherwise the benefits would be lost. Consult with your individual tax advisor and consider the examples below:

Tax Planning Example 1

John and Mary, each over 55 years old, each own a residence and neither has previously elected to exclude any gain. They have decided to get married, sell their respective homes, and move into a retirement community.

Proper tax planning calls for *completion* of both sales *before* they marry. In this way, each of them can claim a separate $125,000 exclusion. If either or both of them *wait* to sell until after marriage, only one sale will be eligible for the exclusion, whether they file separate or joint returns.

Tax Planning Example 2

Herman and Sarah are also planning to marry and both are over 55 years old. Herman has already taken advantage of the $125,000 exclusion on the sale of a residence he formerly owned, but Sarah has not. Sarah should sell her home *before* she and Herman marry; if she does not, her gain will not be eligible for the $125,000 exclusion.

Tax Planning Example 3

Henry elected to exclude gain on the sale of his residence at a time when he was married to Wilma. As required by the regulations, Wilma joined in the election made on their joint return. Wilma later divorces Henry and marries Howard. Neither Wilma nor Howard may make an exclusion election so long as they remain married to each other.

Trap

An individual who joins in an election made by his or her spouse, even if there is no personal benefit, will lose the ability to make his or her own election at a later date and will also cause any future spouse to lose the benefit.

Application with Rollover Rules

A taxpayer who can exclude only a part of his or her gain realized, because of the $125,000 limit on the exclusion, may exclude the balance by making a qualifying rollover. For purposes of determining how much must be reinvested to defer all gain, the selling price of the residence is reduced by $125,000.

Rollover Application Example

Grace, a qualifying taxpayer, sells a house for $240,000 in which her adjusted basis was $90,000. She elects to exclude $125,000 of her $150,000 gain. She may defer the balance of the gain by purchasing a new house, provided that its cost is at least $115,000 ($240,000 minus the $125,000 exclusion).

Because of the once-in-a-lifetime nature of this exclusion, tax-payers must plan to use it intelligently. It probably does not pay to exclude a small gain on the sale of property if there is any chance that a larger one will be realized later. Also, if the tax-payer intends to purchase a new home that will cost as much, or nearly so, as the selling price of the old one, it would normally be advisable to refrain from making the election for this sale.

Questions and Answers on the Exclusion

The exclusion is not difficult to understand. What's difficult is applying it in the many different situations that people find themselves in. The following "Q & A" section will answer many of these:

Question.   *When, exactly, is a person 55 years old?*
Answer.   The law actually interprets you to be 55 one day *before* your fifty-fifth birthday.

Question.   *For the past 3 years, I've gone on a vacation for a couple of months during the summer and rented out my house each time. Since I've only owned my house for a total of 3 years, I need all the time of ownership to qualify under the 3-out-of-the-last-5-years rule. Do the vacations I took disqualify me, particularly since I rented out the property?*
Answer.   No, you may still claim the exclusion. The general rule is that you may take a vacation for up to several months each year. Even if you rent out the subject property during your vacation period, you are still considered to be technically occupying it as a residence.

Question.   *What about absences for longer periods of time. What if a teacher goes on a sabbatical for a year and rents out the subject house the entire time. Can he or she still use that year as qualifying time?*
Answer.   No, probably not. Generally speaking the IRS says that if you're gone for such an extended period of time, you could not claim the house during that year. The rule is that if you stay away more than a couple of months, you "break the

chain" of possession. This matter is in a gray area and may be challengeable in tax court.

Question. *If I have two homes, one a vacation home, can I claim either for the purposes of the exclusion?*

Answer. The rule says that you can take the exclusion only on your principal residence, or your "main home." You can only have one and for the purposes of the $125,000 exclusion, you must have maintained it as your main residence for 3 out of the last 5 years.

Question. *Can the exclusion be taken if I own a condo or a duplex in which I live in one side?*

Answer. Yes. Many types of homes satisfy the principal residence requirement including condos, duplexes, co-ops, and even mobile homes.

If you own a duplex you can claim only that portion of the property in which you reside. If it happens to be an identical duplex, the calculation would be very simple. You could exclude up to one-half of the gain on sale, or $125,000, whichever is less.

Question. *I sell my property and my gain only comes to $90,000; can I take that entire amount even though it's less than $125,000? What happens to the $35,000? Can I claim it later?*

Answer. The exclusion is for "up to" $125,000. If your gain is only $90,000, you can claim the full amount. However, the exclusion is for "only once in a lifetime." Hence if you take the $90,000 now, you forfeit any chance to take the unused $35,000 at a later time.

Question. *Must the subject property be residential? What about commercial property?*

Answer. The rule is that the property must be your principal residence, your main home. If you're using a portion of a commercial property as a residence and you otherwise qualify, that portion may be excluded.

Question. *If the portion of our principal residence is only 40 percent of the total building area, do we only claim 40 percent of $125,000?*

Answer. No. You first determine the total amount of your gain that applies to your personal residence. If you otherwise qualify, you then apply that amount to the full exclusion. For example, the entire property may have a gain of $300,000. Your 40 percent used as a main home would represent $120,000. You can exclude the entire $120,000 but, of course, will be taxed on $180,000.

Question. *What about a trade? Can a home be traded and the seller still claim the exclusion?*

Answer. Yes. A trade, for proposes of the exclusion, is treated as if it were a sale of your old house and purchase of a new one. If you otherwise qualify, you may claim the exclusion on your gain.

Question. *What if one spouse is 55 or older, but the other spouse is younger than 55?*

Answer. The couple qualifies. Only one spouse is required to be 55 under the age qualification. However, both spouses must claim the exclusion jointly.

Question. *If, prior to marriage, a woman took the exclusion on a house, then married a man who had never taken the exclusion, when he turns 55, can they take it as a couple?*

Answer. No. If the current property is owned as community property or as joint tenancy or in some other form of tenancy by entirety, both spouses must join in the choice to exclude. If one previously had already done so, they could not do so now. If, however, the man divorces, never having taken the exclusion, he may later take it on a house he owns entirely.

Question. *Can the exclusion be revoked?*

Answer. Yes. Perhaps you took the exclusion earlier and were able to only save a fraction of the $125,000. Now you have the opportunity to claim the entire amount.

You normally can revoke the exclusion during the same time period you have for claiming a refund on your taxes. That is usually 3 years from the date of filing of the return for the year of the sale or April 15th, whichever is later. If you revoke the exclusion, you must pay tax on the capital gain which you avoided originally by taking the exclusion. Interest on the money may also have to be paid.

Further, all those who entered into the exclusion must agree to revoking it. If you were married when you took the exclusion and are now divorced, both you and your former spouse must still agree to the revocation.

Question. *Can a couple double its exclusion by divorcing?*

Answer. Yes. Prior to the divorce (including an interlocutory decree), both spouses must join in the exclusion. After the final divorce decree is in effect, however, each person would be considered unmarried and could claim up to $125,000.

Question. *If one spouse dies, can the other claim the exclusion on property that they jointly owned?*

Answer. The answer here is complex and usually requires the services of a tax attorney to make recommendation based on the specific circumstances. Generally, the ownership and use qualifications for both the surviving and the dead spouse must be determined for 3 years after the death of one, even though the survivor acquires full title to the property.

To understand the rule, you have to realize that, in general, where a couple has "co-owned" property at the time of the death of one, whether as joint tenants, tenants by entirety, community property, or tenants in common, the tax law regards the single house as two separate properties which we can call Hal's half and Wanda's half.

If you live in a community property state and held the house as community property when Hal dies, both halves of the house get a "stepped-up" basis equal to fair market value at the time of death or, in some cases, shortly thereafter. Since the basis is stepped-up, the taxable gain is reduced without regard to the special $125,000 exclusion. If the house is not sold for much more than that "date of death value," it would be unwise to make the election. In some cases, however, substantial appreciation could occur between the date of death and the date of sale, and it may be desirable to make the exclusion.

As an example, if the husband, Hal, dies, the basic principle is that Wanda's half qualifies for the election if at the time of sale she is over 55 years old, has owned her half for 3 of the past 5 years, and has used the house as her principal residence during that period. Hal's half qualifies for the election only if at the date of sale Wanda is over 55 and Hal had (1) owned his half of the property and (2) occupied it as his principal residence for 3 of the 5 years before the date of sale (not the date of his death). If the parties had owned the house and lived in it for 3 years prior to death and the sale is made within 2 years of Hal's death, the requirements will normally be met on both halves and both halves qualify for the election. The main problem would be if Hal had made an election on another residence which was in force at his death; in such case, Hal's half would not qualify for the election. Also, if Wanda is remarried at the time of the sale, Hal's half doesn't qualify.

If the sale is more than 2 years after Hal dies, Hal's half would not qualify for the election. Hal obviously cannot meet the 3-out-of-5-year test, since he won't have been alive for 3 of the past 5 years. In such a case, only Wanda's half might qualify for the exclusion. Whether one half or both halves qualify, the maximum amount of the exclusion remains $125,000; also, if both halves qualify, Wanda's election will apply to both halves.

Note: If Wanda waits more than 3 years after Hal's death to sell the house, she individually will usually have (1) owned the entire house and (2) occupied it as her residence for 3 of the 5 years prior to sale. Accordingly, her entire gain qualifies for the exclusion and Hal's status is irrelevant. Problems can arise, of course, if Wanda moves out of the house before selling it. The danger area is thus a sale between 2 and 3 years after Hal's death.

Again assuming a community property state, if the parties held the property "as joint tenants" rather than as community property, only Hal's half and not Wanda's half gets a steeped up basis at Hal's death. Thus the exclusion may well be more important since there is a greater taxable gain to be concerned about. However, all the other rules mentioned still apply. Qualification for both halves must be determined separately until Wanda's period of sole ownership is at least 3 years and Hal's half can't qualify once 2 years pass from the date of his death. The 2- to 3-year interval is very dangerous.

In some cases the deceased spouse may have owned the residence as his or her separate property which passes to the surviving spouse by will or intestate succession. This can even occur in a community property state, particularly in the case of people who marry late in life. Where the deceased spouse was the sole owner for income tax purposes, until the survivor can individually qualify for a 3-year holding and use period, qualification for an exclusion requires that (1) the survivor is at least 55 years old at the time of sale and has not remarried, (2) the decedent satisfied the ownership and use requirements for 3 of the 5 years preceding the sale, and (3) the decedent had not made a previous election. This means usually, but not always, that the entire gain will qualify for the exclusion if the sale is made within 2 or more than 3 years after the decedent dies, but it will not qualify if it occurs in the interim period. Furthermore, where the decedent was the sole owner of the house at the time of death, the entire property qualifies for a stepped-up basis, so the exclusion is generally less important.

While the preceding discussion may seem complex, please note that the law is very complex at this point. We emphasize again that professional advice is indispensable if you are actually confronted with one of these situations.

Question. Can the executor of an estate claim the exclusion for the benefit of a deceased?

Answer. Probably not. In general, an executor cannot make the exclusion claim on the behalf of the deceased if it is the executor who sells the house. The executor cannot do it even if the deceased fully qualified, even if he or she entered into a contract of the sale prior to his dying. However, in analogous situations, some courts have overruled the IRS.

It should be noted, however, that if the decedent had not entered into a binding contract to sell the property before his or her death, but had listed the property with a broker, or if the contract were subject to numerous unfulfilled conditions when death occurred, the basis of the property would be "stepped-up" to its fair market value on the date of death and there would be no gain to report.

On the other hand, if the sale was completed prior to death, the exclusion may be claimed on the decedent's final tax return. Either the executor or another person may have been appointed executor or administrator by a probate court. In this case, the final return including the election has to be made by the duly authorized representative, either individually or by joining in a final joint return. If no probate was required, the surviving spouse may file the final return (including a joint return) on behalf of the deceased and claim the election.

Question.   *Do single men and women get half the exclusion?*

Answer.   As noted elsewhere in this chapter, the exclusion is for $125,000, married or single.

Question.   *What if there are several owners of a house who are not spouses? Can they qualify for the exclusion?*

Answer.   Brothers and sisters may own property together as may people who are not linked by blood. Where the house is not community property (no marriage involved) and when it is not owned in entirety or as joint tenants, individual owners do not have to join with one another to get the exclusion. In other words, upon sale those owners who qualify may take the full $125,000 each. Those who do not qualify, do not get any exclusion.

Question.   *I understand that at one time there was another kind of exclusion. Can someone who claimed this earlier exclusion, also claim the current one?*

Answer.   Prior to July 27, 1978, a person who was 65 years of age or older and who had lived in a principal residence for 5 out of eight years could have qualified for an exclusion up to $35,000. Those who took that exclusion can nevertheless also claim the current $125,000 exclusion.

Question.   *Does condemnation qualify as a sale on which the exclusion can apply?*

Answer.   If a house is condemned, that qualifies as a sale. In fact, you may not need to have lived in the condemned house for 3 out of 5 years. The condemnation can shorten the qualification period since it was involuntary. Check with your tax advisor for specifics.

6
Tax Treatment of Rental Real Estate

Determining the tax treatment of rental real estate is a very challenging and difficult task under today's rules. As a result of "antitax shelter" legislation enacted over the past 15 years, and repeatedly strengthened by Congress, the process has become very complex.

To begin, one must initially determine the operating income or loss for each separate rental property owned or sold during the year. If the result for some, or all properties, is an operating loss, special limitations on the deductibility of overall losses from real estate then come into play and must be applied.

The problem is perhaps most difficult in the context of properties that are partially used for rental and partially used for personal purposes of the taxpayer or family members. Before exploring the difficulties involved with overall losses and part-personal properties, let's first lay out the basic "traditional" ground rules for determining the status of receipts, outlays, and depreciation. We'll then discuss the special problem areas.

Receipts

The basic form of gross income is rent receipts. Cash rents are taxable as ordinary income when received, even if they represent prepaid rental income. Security deposits that are refundable at the termination of a lease unless damage to the leased property is found are not considered rent for this purpose, whether or not the landlord must pay interest to the tenant on the deposits.

Improvements

Improvements made by a tenant to leased property are normally not taxable income, either when they are installed or when the lease terminates and the landlord retakes possession of the improved property.

Tenant Paying Landlord's Obligations

If a lease requires the tenant to pay amounts that are the landlord's legal obligation (e.g., property taxes or insurance premiums), the payments to the recipient are treated as additional rental income to the landlord. Normally, however, the landlord can deduct the amounts paid on his or her behalf by the tenant, so the net effect is usually a "wash."

Outlays

The tax treatment of outlays is more difficult. Costs incurred by a landlord may have any of four different tax treatments:

1. Immediate deductibility
2. Capitalization and inclusion in the basis of depreciable assets (*depreciation*)
3. Capitalization and inclusion in the basis of nondepreciable assets
4. Treatment as nondeductible "personal expenses"

Establishing which treatment applies to a particular type of expenditure is often very difficult, although there are some broad general guidelines set out in the law, regulations, and cases in this area.

Deductible versus Capitalized

The general dividing line between a deductible expense and an expenditure that must be capitalized (treated as or added to the basis of an asset) is whether or not the expense is reasonably expected to produce economic values beyond the taxable year in which it is made.

Tip

"Capitalized" means that the cost increases the property's basis as opposed to being deductible in the current year.

Depreciable versus Nondepreciable

The general dividing line between depreciable or amortizable assets on the one hand and nondepreciable assets on the other is whether the asset in question has a finite useful life that is reasonably ascertainable.

Tip

"Amortizable" means that the asset is written off over term of ownership of the property or an arbitrary period such as 5 years (when permitted or required by the tax law) as opposed to "depreciable" which means that the asset is written off over its own life.

Nondeductible Personal versus Business Related

The general dividing line between nondeductible personal expenditures on the one hand and business-related costs on the other is whether the purpose and effect of the expenditure relates, primarily, to current or future income or to personal benefits for the person making the expenditure or for family members.

Unfortunately, these broad principles are too general to decide most "close cases," and a great number of more specific rules have been developed by Congress, the IRS, and the Courts which draw the line at one point or another. Unfortunately also, these more specific rules are often changed by legislation, regulations, or new court decisions; therefore, certainty is almost impossible to achieve.

In the specific area of costs related to income-producing real estate, some of the most important specific rules that have developed follow.

Cost of Land. The cost of acquiring land is a nondeductible and nondepreciable capital expenditure which can be recovered only upon sale or disposition of the land. The cost of acquiring or improving buildings and structures is generally a depreciable capital expenditure, recoverable over the recovery period specified in the tax law.

You can allocate between land and improvements based on reasonable judgment, which should, however, be backed up by some type of objective estimate, such as an insurance company appraisal. You don't have to use the allocation found on the property tax bill.

Ordinary Repairs. Ordinary repairs are currently deductible, but costs that improve or better property must be capitalized and added to the basis of the property improved. When deciding what is a repair and what is an improvement, consider the following quotation from Section 1.162-4 of the Income Tax Regulations:

> The cost of incidental repairs which neither materially add to the value of the property nor appreciably prolong its life, but keep it in an ordinarily efficient operating condition, may be deducted as an expense....Repairs in the nature of replacements, to the extent that they arrest deterioration and appreciably prolong the life of the property shall...be capitalized and depreciated....

Depreciation

The cost of buildings and structural components must be written off in accordance with specified methods. Under current law:

Commercial real estate.   Commercial real estate acquired after 1985 and before May 13, 1993, has a useful life of 31.5 years.

Residential real estate.   Residential real estate has a life of 27.5 years.

These lives are used regardless of whether the taxpayer is a "first user" of the building, or has purchased it from a prior owner.

Tip

The new tax law (1993) increases the depreciable life of commercial real estate to 39 years, effective for property acquired or placed in service on or after May 13, 1993.

Buildings Acquired Before 1986

Buildings acquired before 1986 are eligible for somewhat faster depreciation, in some cases as short as 15 years, in others 18 or 19 years, depending on the precise date of acquisition.

Depreciating Land Improvements

Land improvements that are not part of a building or structural component may be depreciated over 15 years. Typical examples include fencing, paving, landscaping, and sprinklers. Not only can these items be deducted over a shorter period, they can also be depreciated using a so-called accelerated method, which allows larger deductions in the earlier years. The IRS has published tables giving the percentage of cost that can be deducted as depreciation in each year of a property's holding. Of course, if you sell the property, you offset any remaining basis against the proceeds of sale.

Component Method of Depreciation

Under current law, taxpayers may not use the so-called component method of depreciation, which assigns separate lives to the various components of a structure (roof, heating system, elevators, etc.). All structural components, whenever purchased or installed, are subject to the 27.5- or 39-year periods described above. Some special-purpose structures designed as adjuncts to machinery are not considered buildings and are eligible for faster write-offs. Because of the complexity of these rules, taxpayers who think that they may be applicable should consult a professional advisor.

Examples of structural components are built-in heating, lighting, or air-conditioning systems; permanent walls, ceilings, pipes, and ducts; plumbing and plumbing fixtures; and electric wiring and affixed lighting fixtures. In a few cases, movable partitions, overhead doors, and other relatively easily removable items have been held, by courts, not to be structural components for purposes of the former investment credit. These decisions should also apply for purposes of deciding what items are not components of a building for depreciation purposes.

Shorter Depreciable Lives

True personal property usually qualifies for write-off over 7 years. The only assets most ordinary owners of real estate own that qualify for the shorter 5-year write-off are computers and peripheral devices, automobiles, and light duty trucks. However, these are all "listed property," which means that limitations on the deduction apply unless more than half of the total use during a year is for business (including rental) purposes.

Seven-year depreciation is the "default state." That is to say, if there is an item of personal property that IRS rulings do not treat as having a specific life, its life will be considered 7 years. There are no guideline lives for residential furniture and furnishings, so this property, if owned by a landlord, will be depreciated over 7 years. Office furniture and furnishings are depreciated over 7 years.

Depreciating Roof Repairs

New roofs are structural components and are treated as separate improvements having a 27.5-year life (up to 39 years for nonresidential property). Repair of a roof gets into the gray area. Our view is that 40 percent replacement is still a repair, not an improvement, but there is no clear cut rule on this.

Tip

Another example is carpeting. Nailed-down wall-to-wall carpeting is a structural component, but the IRS has held that some types of carpeting, affixed less permanently, are not. The real questions are whether the carpeting (1) can be removed without damage to the floor below it and (2) once removed, can be reused at another location. If these are answered Yes, the carpet may qualify for 7-year depreciation. This was the test that the IRS used to separate property that qualified for investment tax credit from that which didn't.

Depreciation in the Year of Acquisition

The depreciation deduction applicable to buildings and structural components must be prorated, using a mid-month convention. For example, you take 3½ months of depreciation for the year of acquisition if you closed escrow during the month of September.

The general rule for personal property is that half a year's depreciation can be taken in the year of acquisition, regardless of whether the purchase was in January or November. That is the half-year convention.

However, there is a special antiabuse rule. If property placed into service during the last 3 months of the taxable year exceeds 40 percent of the total cost of property placed in service during the whole year, you use the mid-quarter convention for all property placed in service during the year. In effect, you get only an eighth-year depreciation in the year of acquisition for property placed in service after October 1.

Alternative System of Depreciation

If property is located outside the United States or was financed with tax-exempt bonds under applicable provisions of the law, depreciation must be taken over a period of 40 years. In addition, the 40-year life is used to determine allowable depreciation for purposes of the alternative minimum tax (AMT). The AMT is basically a second-stage tax calculation in which the rate is lower (26 percent or in some cases 28 percent currently), but the "base" is larger because deductions and exclusions, and some deferrals, are either not allowed at all or are allowed only on a more limited basis than for purposes of the "regular tax."

Trap

Some tax book writers have suggested that property owners may deduct all of the costs of an improvement in the year of purchase by using Section 179. (This section, basically, allows the rapid depreciation of some items purchased for use in a business.) This is bad advice because Section 179 only applies to personal property, while a building improvement constitutes real property.

True personal property is only assets that are not permanently affixed to a land or a structure, that can be removed without damage to the structure, and that can be reused after removal. Even for these items—such as furniture and appliances—there are two requirements for the Section 179 deduction that will be difficult for most real estate investors to meet. First, the property must be used in the *active* conduct of a trade or business," rather than just in the conduct of a trade or business. Further, if the income from the property is derived by leasing or renting it, two requirements must be satisfied in addition (unless the lessor is a corporation):

First, the term of the lease must be less than 50 percent of the property's class life (which will often be satisfied). Second, and much harder, in the first year that the property is operated, the taxpayer's ordinary and necessary business expenses relating to the property (not including depreciation and interest, but including insurance, etc.) must be at least 15 percent of the rental income produced by the property in that period.

In most cases, we think that this test is not going to be easy to meet. (One exception might be coin-operated washers and dryers. However, in most cases, these are owned by independent laundry companies who just pay rent to the landlord of the building and, hence, do not qualify.)

As a practical matter, we believe that landlords rarely if ever claim Section 179 first-year deductions for their personal property because the 15 percent expense test is so difficult to meet.

Costs Incurred in Financing

Most costs incurred in acquiring financing must be capitalized and written off on the straight-line method over the term of the financing. If the taxpayer pays off a loan early (e.g., by refinancing), unamortized loan costs are deductible at the time of payoff.

Interest

Interest is normally deductible, if property is held for income-producing purposes, including anticipated gain on sale. However, most interest paid during the construction period of property must be capitalized and added to the basis of the property under construction. These rules are very complex, and professional advice must be obtained by anyone involved in a construction or improvement project. Also, prepaid interest may be deducted only over the term for which it is prepaid. (See also a discussion of interest deduction in Chapter 3.)

Insurance Premiums

Insurance premiums are generally deductible, except for any premium paid for coverage beyond the end of the year in which payment is made. Prepaid premiums can only be deducted over the period to which they relate.

Real Estate Taxes

Real estate taxes paid for general government support are

deductible when paid. However, special assessments for localized benefits (e.g., sidewalks, street lights, or landscaping) are not deductible and are added to the cost basis of the property burdened by them.

Payments to Family Members

For tax purposes, an attractive option is to employ your children or grandchildren to do work around the rental property, such as yard maintenance and clean-up, setting out trash, and the like. You can deduct the reasonable wages that you pay them, thereby shifting income to lower-rate taxpayers. This is considered earned income, so it's not subject to the "kiddie tax," in the case of children under 14. (Under the "kiddie tax," unearned income in excess of about $1000 per year is taxed at the parent's rate until the child reaches as 14.) "Unearned income" is basically the same as "portfolio income," that is, interest and dividends, but it also includes rents.

If you employ children under 18, or low-tax-bracket parents, you will not have to pay social security taxes, but this relief does not extend to grandchildren. There will be required income tax withholding if the payments exceed the appropriate withholding exemptions claimed by the child or parent.

Management Fees

These are usually deductible, unless they are prepaid for a period extending past the end of the year. If they are, the portion attributable to future periods must in effect be capitalized and recovered only over the term for which they are paid.

Legal Expenses and Damages

The basis test for deducting attorney's fees, costs of suit, and any settlements or judgments paid is the "origin and character" test. If the claim in respect of which the expenses or damages were incurred arose in the ordinary course of business, the expenses are deductible. If, however, the claim is one that goes to title, for example, an individual asserting that he or she has an interest in property that you claim to own exclusively, any expenses and settlement payments must generally be capitalized (i.e., added to basis and recovered over a separate period of 27.5 or 39 years) to the extent that they protect your rights in buildings. Expenses that protect your rights in land can only be recovered when you sell the land.

For example, the cost of suits against a tenant for nonpayment of rent, or causing damages to the property, would probably be deductible. The cost of suing someone who agreed to sell you property and then "welshed" will be added to the basis of your property if you ultimately do gain title to the property. Suits for additional payments in the case of condemnation would be deducted against the condemnation award received, in general, as a capital gain.

It does not matter that your purpose in defending a lawsuit was to protect your income-producing property from being seized to pay your debts. If the origin of the claim against you was a personal dispute—like a divorce (other than in community property states) or a "brawl"—you won't be able to deduct the costs of defense. However, if the claim against you arose out of your business activities relating to the property, a deduction for part or all of your legal costs would probably be allowed.

Net Loss

If, after application of all of the foregoing rules, your rental property produces an overall "net loss," some additional rules must be dealt with before the taxpayer can deduct that loss against his or her income from other sources (such as salary, interest, or dividend income). The two major limitations are the "at risk" rule and the "passive activity" rule. They are applied in that order.

At Risk Rule

Under the at risk rule, deductions in excess of income realized from a property are allowed only to the extent of the taxpayer's amount at risk. The amount at risk in a property generally equals the taxpayer's cash investment in the property, plus the amount of funds borrowed for use in the acquisition or operation of the property, to the extent that the taxpayer is personally liable. If the taxpayer is not personally liable, borrowed funds are taken into account only to the extent of the basis of other property (not the property in respect of which the loan is made) pledged to the lender as security for payment of the debt. Arrangements under which the taxpayer is protected against loss may limit or eliminate amounts that might otherwise be considered at risk.

Trap

If a taxpayer deducts losses because he or she has a sufficient at risk amount and later the at risk amount is substantially reduced or eliminated (e.g., by conversion of recourse debt to nonrecourse debt), deductions previously allowed may be recaptured as income.

Tip

An important exception to the at risk rule is that "qualified nonrecourse financing" is treated like an amount at risk. (Nonrecourse means that in the event of default, the borrower is not personally liable for the loss.) Such financing must be made by an institutional lender, rather than the seller of the property. Under some circumstances, loans made by a related party to the borrower (such as a parent) can be treated as qualified nonrecourse financing, if the terms are comparable to those imposed by unrelated lenders.

Applying Passive Activity Rules

The passive activity rules are probably the most difficult of all the special limitations to apply. Simply filling out the required forms and maintaining the numerous worksheets prescribed by the instructions is an extremely complex undertaking. See Chapter 8 for a detailed explanation of passive/active rules.

Mixed-Use Property

If property is partially used for personal purposes as a principal residence and partially for operating a business or as a source of rental income, a number of special rules come into play.

If the uses can be divided spatially, such as where the taxpayer occupies one unit in a building as a residence and rents out the other during the entire year, occupancy costs must be allocated in proportion to the value of the respective portions of the property. Only the portion of maintenance, insurance, and utilities that relates to the rental portion is deductible. Interest and taxes must also be prorated because even though they are generally allowed as deductions regardless of the use to which property is put, there are special limitations on itemized deductions to which the personal portion of these expenses is subject.

Home Office

Special limitations apply to business use of a taxpayer's home, most notably "home offices." Under a recent decision of the United States Supreme Court, home office deductions that are claimed by someone who works as an employee will probably be disallowed altogether unless the taxpayer proves that he or she spends more time in the home office than he or she does at all other business locations combined. (See also Chapter 3 for more information.)

Furthermore, it will be very difficult for employees who are furnished work space by the employer to justify any deduction for home offices. With rare exceptions, home office deductions probably should not be claimed by employees—putting them on the tax return will be a very tempting invitation for the IRS to audit the affected items (and perhaps others as well).

For self-employed persons, including a "secondary business," the rules are considerably more liberal. Your can deduct office expenses, within strict limits, if your use of the home office is in any one of the following categories:

1. It is the principal place of business for any trade or business that you conduct.
2. It is regularly used by patients, clients, or customers for face-

to-face meetings with the owner of the business.

3. It is located in a separate structure, such as a detached garage, and is merely used "in connection" with your (nonemployee) business.

Also, the use must be exclusive and regular. You can't just sporadically have meetings in a room that is otherwise totally unused. Also, you can't deduct a portion of the costs of a dining room or den because some of the time you conduct business there.

A few categories of business use are exempt from the exclusive use requirement. If you regularly sell products as an independent dealer or distributor, you can deduct costs allocable to space used to store your inventory but only if your home is the sole fixed location of your selling business.

Expenses attributable to rental income from your home can be deducted without regard to the exclusive use requirement. So, for example, you can rent out your home for a portion of the year, while you are away, and can deduct costs even though part of the time the home was used personally. Also, your income from a "boarder" can be offst by deductions even if both you and the boarder use some of the space in the home.

Also, if you have a licensed day care business in your home, you can deduct expenses allocable to space that you use both in the business and personally. This applies if you provide day care for children, for persons over the age of 65, or for persons who are unable to care for themselves.

However, your expenses must be allocated based on the ratio that the total days or hours of business use bears to the total number of days or hours in the year that the space is available for use for any purpose. Thus, if space is sometimes used for day care and sometimes for personal purposes and sometimes is totally unused, the unused time reduces the amount deductible.

Where you are permitted to deduct expenses for a home office, you will still be subject to a number of limitations and restrictions. First, you have to make a reasonable allocation of expenses to the office location. Items like insurance can probably be allocated on a space basis (although extra premiums charged just because business use occurs would probably be fully deductible). For maintenance, you could deduct costs entirely if they are solely attributable to the home office or work space and allocate them in other situations based on space ratios or possibly some other reasonable approach.

If your expenses pass all of the foregoing tests, you still may encounter deduction problems. As a general rule, you cannot create a "loss" by deducting expenses of your at-home business. If the sum of (1) generally allowable expenses for items other than interest and taxes plus (2) the portion of your deductions for interest and taxes that are allocable to the "business portion" of your home exceeds the gross income attributable to your at-home business, you can't write them off against, say, salary, interest, or dividend income. The net loss must be carried forward and deducted only against future net income from your at-home business.

For example, assume that Mr. Smith incurs total maintenance, insurance, and utilities expense at his home of $8000; that his interest expense totals $24,000, and his real estate taxes are $2000. Assume that he appropriately determines that 20 percent of these expenses are properly allocable to the space in which he conducts a business and that the space qualifies as his principal place of business. His gross income, less expenses other than those attributable to the home office, is $6000. His total allocable expenses are $34,000, and 20 percent of that is $6800. Only $6000 of the expenses are deductible this year; the remaining $800 must be carried forward and deducted only against future profits from the same business.

7

Vacation Homes and Other Secondary Residences

Vacation homes and other secondary residences, for either the owners themselves or members of their family, create many special tax traps and a few opportunities.

First, it's important to remember that you won't be able to use the two major tax benefits available to owners of a principal residence when you sell them: neither the rollover rule nor the $125,000 exclusion. The reason, quite simply, is that the vacation property is unquestionably *not* your principal residence.

On the other hand, you will be able to claim interest deductions under the residence rules for debt attributable to a second home (any one that you select). This only applies to one second home, however, not to your third, fourth, or fifth home or any property that you do not personally occupy.

Mixed Use

Most problems occur when the taxpayer uses a property for personal purposes some of the time and rents it out at other times during the year. This is a very common situation since many who have a second home count on rental income part of the time to pay the home's expenses. It's important to remember, however, that when there is personal use part of the time, the rules that were used for rental property explained in Chapter 6 must give way to the special rules for vacation homes given here. (Another difficult situation is where you permit members of your family to occupy homes—for instance, you buy a condominium for your college student child to occupy. This will be discussed later in this chapter.)

Trap

One general rule is that if you have an operating loss on property that is also used for personal purposes, *it cannot be deducted at all*, either in the current year or on a carry-forward basis.

The 14-Day Rule

The restrictions on overall losses not being used to offset other income don't apply where the taxpayer's use during the year is less than the *greater* of (1) 14 days or (2) 10 percent of the number of days that the property is rented at a fair rental.

Example 1. John's ski condominium was actually rented out at a fair rental for 135 days. John and his family used the condo for 10 days total during the year. Because his personal use did not exceed 14 days, he may write off losses against other income (subject, however, to two other restrictions described later, the investment interest restriction and the passive loss restriction.)

Example 2. Pat's resort condominium was actually rented for 215 days. She and her family could make personal use of the condominium for up to 21 days without being subject to the vacation home restrictions on deductibility.

Repairs and Maintenance

Days that you spend at the vacation home for bona fide repairs or maintenance are not counted as personal use days, even if you also ski or hike or whatever at the site during the latter part of the day, so long as your *primary* activity is repair or maintenance. A logbook to record use of the home would be a very good idea.

Rented for Less Than 15 Days

On the other hand, if the unit is actually rented for less than 15 days, income from the rental need not be reported, and all expenses are treated as nondeductible (other than interest and taxes).

Example.   Phyllis rented out her New Orleans home for 12 days during Mardi Gras and collected $2000 in rent. None of this needs to be reported as gross income.

Trap

Use of property by members of a taxpayer's family is generally treated the same as use by the taxpayer personally.

Tip

There is a very important exception to the rule listed in "Trap" above. If the unit is rented at a fair rental, the taxpayer may deduct any excess losses incurred in the year, subject to the passive activity and possibly the investment interest limitations. This can include rental to a child or grandchild or other family members.

Ownership Interests

The law also says that restrictions on deductibility of losses apply if the property is occupied by someone with an ownership interest in the unit, even if he or she is not otherwise related to the owner. It is hard to see what justification exists for this rule, in the unrelated party situation.

Equity Sharing

However, and again importantly, equity sharing arrangements, in which the financing party charges a fair rent to the co-owning and occupying family, escape some of the personal use disallowance rule, though not the passive activity disallowance rule.

The 12-Month Rule

If a principal residence is rented out for a period in excess of 12 months, or for a period of less than 12 months at the end of which the unit is sold or exchanged, and a fair rental is charged, the restrictions on losses don't apply for the period of the year during which the qualifying rental occurs.

Example. Professor Jones takes a sabbatical leave starting in September. Her house is rented out from September 15 through the beginning of the next academic year. If her tenants stay for at least 1 year, through September 14 of the next year, she will be able to deduct losses on the rental, provided that it is a fair rental.

Personal and Income-Producing Use

If the same unit of property is used during the year for both personal and income-producing activities (a common example being a resort area condominium that is placed in a "rental pool" for some part of the year and is used by the owner as a vacation home for other parts of the year) not covered by the 14-day or 10 percent of time rule, other complex restrictions on deductibility come into play.

Allocating Expenses

In addition to the prohibition on deducting net losses, taxpayers who use their property for both rental and personal purposes during a year must properly allocate their expenses against the rental income. Expenses allocable to the personal use period, other than interest and taxes, are not deductible at all.

Expenses must first be allocated based on the number of days which the property is used for personal and income-producing purposes. For vacation homes, "vacant days," when the property is not used at all, are ignored in computing the amount.

Assume that $20,000 in operating expenses must be allocated. The taxpayer uses his or her vacation home for 30 days, and it is rented out at a fair rental for 90 days. Twenty-five percent of this amount, or $5000, is allowable as a deduction against the rental income.

Trap

As a general rule, taxpayers cannot deduct the "rental loss" on personal use property against other income they realize. Moreover, interest and taxes that are generally deductible without limit (for rental properties) must be used to offset rental income, not just other expenses (such as fuel, insurance, and maintenance) that are deductible only against rental income. Again, it is important to note that the maximum amount of deductions for all types of expenses other than interest and taxes is the rental income from the property less the properly allocated interest and tax deductions.

Tax Consequences in Equity-Sharing Agreements

Sometimes equity-sharing agreements are entirely "business deals," where the financing party agrees to make most or all of the down payment on property in exchange for a return including rental income and a share of any profit on sale. Equally often, however, the parties to the agreement are bound by ties of blood or friendship, and the financing parties feel that they are "helping out" their children, grandchildren, nieces, or nephews to acquire a house.

Normally, in these arrangements, the occupying party pays all, or nearly all of the occupancy costs, including interest and property taxes. The major deduction sought by the occupying party is depreciation.

Although it is theoretically possible for these arrangements to provide a net loss that could be deducted against other income, the passive loss rules will usually be a barrier to an unlimited deduction, except for the $25,000 allowance provided to moderate-income taxpayers (see Chapter 6 for further information). In fact, it is questionable whether the typical equity-sharing arrangement will involve the kind of active participation necessary for allowance of even this limited relief.

When the occupying parties pay all of the interest and taxes, even though they have only a partial interest in the property, they can deduct all of their payments. Under established case law, a tenant in common may deduct all of the payments he or she makes, notwithstanding that he or she may have a right of reimbursement from other owners. (In fact, the agreement relating to the equity-sharing arrangement should negate any such right of reimbursement).

8

Passive and Active Rules

In 1986 under the Tax Reform Act, the government significantly changed the rules for deductions on real estate. It introduced the concepts of active and passive activities. The effect, for many people, was to make it impossible to offset losses in real estate investments against ordinary income from wages or self-employment or from interest and dividends on securities, bank accounts, or government bonds or from capital gains from selling securities at a profit. (Note: There is an exclusion which may apply to you which we'll discuss shortly.)

These rules, briefly, state that all real estate investment activity produces "passive income" or "passive loss." Most ordinary income is either "active income" or "portfolio income." You cannot offset passive losses against either category of income.

This was a telling blow against those who owned substantial real estate investments and had been using losses (generated in large part through depreciation—a loss primarily on "paper") to offset their ordinary income. Particularly hard hit were high-income taxpayers with large or many properties. Unfortunately, it also had a strong effect on the average person who might own one or two rental homes and might be prevented from writing off this loss in the current year as well.

Tip

Thus, a special exclusion of up to $25,000 was created which applied to low- to middle-income wage earners. The rules are fairly complex but not impossibly so.

Definitions

Active.   Income from an activity such as a trade or business in which the taxpayer is a material participant. For example, wages earned from an employer are considered active. Income derived from self-employment is likewise considered active.

Passive.   Income (or loss) from an activity in which the taxpayer is not a material participant. This includes tax shelters. Real estate rental activities are automatically included here.

Portfolio.   Income from securities, such as dividends or interest.

Exceptions

As noted, net losses from a passive activity such as rental real estate are generally disallowed. There are, however, certain exceptions to this rule:

Exception 1

Losses from one passive activity can offset net income from another passive activity.

Passive Offset Example.   Sheila and Henry own two rental homes. The first has a loss of $7000 after depreciation in the current year. They sell the second and realize a gain of $50,000. The $7000 loss on the first property can be used to offset, or reduce, the gain recognized on the second. Thus on the second property the gain recognized will be $43,000.

Gain recognized on property 2	$50,000
Loss recognized on property 1	−7,000
Net income from sales of both	$43,000

Exception 2

Any losses from a given activity that are not used to offset gains from other activities, or gains on the disposition of the activity, are generally "suspended," or deferred. This deferral continues forward until the losses are allowed to be deducted in the year in which the taxpayer terminates his or her involvement with the activity (sells the property), provided that such disposition is one in which gain or loss is *fully* recognized.

If the activity is terminated through a fully taxable disposition to an unrelated party, previously suspended losses may be deducted in the year of such disposition.

Termination of Ownership Example.   In the above example, assume that 4 years later Sheila and Henry sell their one remaining rental property to an unrelated party. It is a straightforward cash deal with no trade or part payment involved. They had been carrying forward $21,000 of suspended loss. They may now write off that loss against any gain from the sale.

If you dispose of a building at a loss, you can still offset the suspending operating losses and in effect deduct them from your ordinary income in the year of sale.

You can also use suspended passive losses against passive income from other properties on a current basis. Thus, if you have suspended passive losses on property 1, and purchase property 2, free and clear of debt, thereby generating taxable profit from property 2, the suspended losses will shelter the profit on property 2 until they are used up.

Exception 3

Up to $25,000 per year of losses incurred in operating rental property are deductible despite the passive loss rules, provided that the taxpayer "actively participates" in the rental activity. Active participation means that the taxpayer makes the major operating decisions about the property, such as establishing rents, approving new tenants, and authorizing major expenditures.

Trap

Most high-income taxpayers suffer a "phaseout" of the $25,000 allowance. The allowance is reduced by 50 cents for each dollar of adjusted gross income in excess of $100,000. At adjusted gross income levels of $150,000 and above, no allowance for active participation losses is permitted. However, these taxpayers can still deduct rental losses against net rental income from other properties, and upon a complete and fully taxable disposition of the property.

Tip

Active participation does not mean that the taxpayer must handle the rental property entirely by him- or herself. A property management firm may be used to handled day-to-day activities, provided that all major operating decisions (such as setting the rental amount, deciding on which tenants to rent to, determining whether to use a lease or month-to-month tenancy, etc.) are forwarded to and made by the taxpayer.

Calculating Adjusted Gross Income for the Exclusion

Some special rules apply to the calculation of adjusted gross income:

Social security benefits are excluded even if they are actually partially taxable.

Interest income on U.S. bonds is included even if it qualifies for an exclusion.

No deduction can be taken for contributions to an IRA.

Passive Activity versus Business Interest

Passive activities include *all* rental activities unless they are subject to certain "recharacterization" rules and business activities in which the taxpayer does not "materially participate." Ownership of income-producing real property is thus, in almost all cases, a passive activity. However, if the activity involves the provision of significant services to customers over and above those normally provided by landlords, as in the case of an operating hotel, motel, or nursing home, the activity is considered a business rather than a rental activity. Likewise, income from property used for very short periods of time by customers, like a golf course or driving range, is not considered rental income. Rent can also be considered incidental to a selling activity, or conduct of a business, if rental income is less than 2 percent of the lesser of (1) the unadjusted basis or (2) the fair market value of the property.

Income from this type of business is active income if the taxpayer materially participates in the activity or satisfies any of six other tests set out in the IRS regulations.

Using Passive Losses Against Business Income

It is sometimes possible to use passive losses against income from a business. This is only possible, however, if the taxpayer did not "materially participate" in the business activity. IRS regulations lay down no fewer than seven separate tests of material participation. Even if none of them applies, in some cases business income will be recharacterized as nonpassive because of "significant participation" by the taxpayer in the year in question or in prior tax years. Taxpayers clearly need professional advice if they want to treat business income, as opposed to rental income, as passive in nature.

The most common test of material participation is devoting 500 hours to participating in the activity for the taxable year. If the 500-hour threshold is not met, but no one other than the taxpayer (including noninvestor employees or contractors hired to work in the activity) participates to any extent in the activity for the year, the second test is satisfied.

If the taxpayer's participation is for at least 100 hours and is at least as great as any other person's (including all employees and contractors), he or she will be considered a material participant.

If the activity is one in which the taxpayer participates for 100 hours and has a similar level of activity in other ventures which, together add up to more than 500 hours of participation, he or she will satisfy the test. Thus, you can't escape material participation by dividing up your activities into a number of small segments.

If you materially participated in an activity for 5 of the past 10 years, your participation will be treated as material this year,

If an activity is a personal service activity, and you materially participated for *any* 3 prior taxable years, whether or not consecutive, you will be deemed a material participant this year. These are typically activities in the fields of professional services—health, law, engineering, architecture, accounting, actuarial science—and in performing arts and "consulting." Thus, semi-retired persons are considered material participants as long as they continue to do any work.

You can almost always escape being categorized as a material participant if your interest is only that of a limited partner, provided that you don't hold another interest as a general partner in the same activity. Also, if you in fact satisfy the 500-hour, 5-out-of-10-prior-years, or any 3 prior-year tests described above, limited partnership status will not exempt you from being held a material participant.

It is important to note that participation of any one spouse will be treated as participation of the other spouse, for purposes of all of the prior rules.

Even if you escape being treated as a material participant, you can still run afoul of "recharacterization rules" laid down by the IRS to thwart taxpayers who may be seeking "passive income generators," sometimes called PIGS.

There are six recharacterization rules. The most important, probably, is that if you have net income from significant participation activities (where you spend more than 100 hours but less than 500 hours of activity during the year), you can't offset that income with passive losses, including rental losses.

Ground rent from unimproved real estate won't constitute passive income. To constitute passive income, at least 30 percent of the *unadjusted* basis, or cost, for a parcel of property must be attributable to the building or other depreciable asset.

An important rule relates to property that the taxpayer, or partnership in which he or she has an interest, constructs and then either rents out or sells. If you materially participate in development of the parcel, including construction activities, and then *use* the property to produce rental income for less than 12 months before selling it, gain will be characterized as active rather than passive.

Use does not commence until the property is ready for rent and all "significant value-enhancing services" have been performed, relating to construction, renovation, or lease up. However, the IRS has indicated that lease-up services will not usually be viewed as value-enhancing.

If you own property and lease it to another entity that conducts a business in which you materially participate, net rental income is not considered passive. This commonly applies when individuals own real estate that is leased to corporations they control, for purposes of carrying on a manufacturing, marketing, or service business.

Under rather complicated rules, net income from an "equity-financed lending activity" and certain types of royalty income received from a controlled taxpayer are recharacterized as non-passive income.

Borrowed Funds

Gains and losses from the sale of passive activity property are generally themselves passive. If funds are borrowed and then invested in a passive activity, both interest expense and income from cancellation or discharge of indebtedness are treated as passive if the borrowed funds are "traceable" to the investment. Taxpayers should maintain records of exactly how they invested borrowed funds in order to maximize the chance of deducting interest expense.

Interest Income

Conversely, interest income is never treated as passive unless the interest is received in the ordinary course of a banking, lending, or finance-type business. Instead, both interest and dividends on corporate stocks are treated as "portfolio income," which cannot be offset by passive activity losses (except in the year that a passive activity terminates).

Death and Suspended Passive Losses

If a taxpayer dies holding property on which he or she had suspended passive losses, the passive losses are deducted on the taxpayer's final return but only to the extent that they exceed the "step up in basis" which the passive activity property may enjoy as a result of the taxpayer's death.

9
Installment Sales

The installment method of accounting is often used to postpone taxes due on the sale of property. However, although it has its place in the world of real estate taxation, at the outset the reader is warned that the authors feel it is not the ideal method of selling property. For one thing, gain is only deferred, not eliminated. In contrast, tax-deferred exchanges can result in permanent elimination of gain if exchanged property is held until the death of the seller (or the first to die of a married couple). For another, the rules are complex and contain a number of traps that must be avoided if even deferral is to be achieved.

Nevertheless, installments sales are used. The following explains the general concept and many of the pitfalls and concerns.

The Concept of an Installment Sale

The concept of an installment sale is simple—rather than pay tax on the value of "paper" taken back by the seller as part of the selling price, the tax is paid proportionally to the collections of principal on the note. In other words, the full tax is not due on the sale of the property. Rather, it is due as the cash is actually received for the sale.

Tip

The installment sale is actually an extension of the usual "cash method."

Illustrating an Installment Sale

To illustrate, suppose that Mr. Brown owns a house in which his "tax basis" is $120,000. (See Chapter 2 for a discussion of how basis is computed.) He sells the home for a gross price of $300,000, payable $50,000 at the time of closing and $250,000 in five equal installments of principal, of $50,000 each, payable annually commencing 1 year after the closing date. Mr. Brown's house is free and clear of obligations. He incurs $20,000 of closing costs, including brokerage commissions.

Tip

Interest is also normally paid with each installment of principal but does not enter into the installment sale calculation so long as it is "adequate."

Mr. Brown's anticipated profit on the sale of the house is $160,000 ($300,000 selling price less $20,000 expenses and $120,000 basis). Under the installment method, this profit is assigned to each installment of principal, in the ratio that the installment bears to the total contract price. Thus, one-sixth of the total profit, that is $26,666.67, is reportable in the year of sale, and an additional one-sixth with each collection of an installment. This is reported as a capital gain, in most cases. (Another way to look at this is that the "profit ratio" of each payment is $160,000/$300,000, or 53.33 percent.) Of course, the collections of interest are ordinary income.

Suppose now that Mr. Brown does not own his house free and clear, but that there is a mortgage on it that the buyer will assume, in the amount of $80,000. The existence of the mortgage loan does not change Mr. Brown's profit, but it does affect his cash collections. Assuming that he still gets a $50,000 down payment, he will only be able to receive $170,000 in the five installments, which will thus be $34,000 each.

As explained in Chapter 2, the fact that there is a mortgage on the property does not change the calculation of taxable gain or profit: The anticipated profit is still $160,000. Under the applicable regulations, this profit is still reported proportionately to collections. Since the total to be collected is now only $220,000, payable $50,000 at once and five annual installments of $34,000 each, the profit calculations are as follows:

Gross profit	$160,000	(a)
Cash to be collected	$220,000	(b)
Profit ratio	72.73%	(a/b)
Taxable given from down payment	$36,365	(a/b × $50,000)
Taxable given from each payment of principal	$24,820	(a/b × $34,000)

When a Loan Is Paid Off

The result would be quite different if the original loan were paid off at closing, rather than being assumed by the buyer. In this situation, the payment of the original loan is considered to be an additional amount paid to the seller. Therefore, the seller's collections in the year of sale are treated as $130,000 rather than $50,000. The profit ratio is 53.33 percent, as in the first example. However, the amount of profit reported in the year of sale is 53.33 percent of $130,000, or $69,433—a lot more than the actual cash collected. The tax on this amount could approach $27,000, using typical federal and state income tax rates.

When Debt Exceeds Tax Basis

Special problems arise when the debt assumed by a buyer *exceeds* the tax basis of the property. Suppose, to use the same general example, that the mortgage assumed by the buyer was $200,000, so that the amount of payments to be received by the seller was only $100,000, payable $20,000 down and then $1700 per month for 5 years, including interest at 10 percent per annum). There is a partial split between the IRS view and the Tax Court cases in this area.

According to the IRS, the excess of mortgage over basis, that is, $80,000 ($200,000 less $120,000), is a taxable gain in the year of sale. All actual cash payments will represent gain. The tax cases don't disagree with this view.

Wraparounds

The conflict comes in connection with "all-inclusive," or "wrap-around," notes used in lieu of a simple assumption of debt by the buyer. Under this type of note, the buyer makes payments to the seller, for an amount which "includes" the balance due on the underlying financing. The seller agrees to make the monthly payments on the underlying financing.

Example. Assume that the $200,000 loan, also at 10 percent, was payable in equal monthly installments of $1843, for a remaining term of 26 years. The buyer agrees to pay the seller $3543 per month for 5 years and $1843 per month thereafter, and the seller agrees to satisfy the underlying mortgage debt with the buyer's payments. Under the case law view of this transaction, the seller's gain can be reported in the following way:

Profit ratio	53.3% (160,000/300,000)
Profit component of initial payments	$1889 (53.33% × 3543)
Capital recovery in initial payments	$1654
Profit component in later payments	$983
Capital recovery in later payments	$860

Notice how this approach defers the tax impact. Of course, in the later years, the seller will keep no cash "in his or her pocket," but more than half of the payments received will constitute taxable gain.

Tip

The IRS will argue that the excess of mortgage over basis is taxable in the initial year of sale, but sellers should not agree to this position, in view of the court cases on point.

Trap

Of course, the buyer must have a considerable degree of trust in the seller so that he or she is sure that there is no risk of the seller running off with payments that are intended to service the underlying debt. The seller should insist that the monthly checks come to him or her first, because if the buyer sent them directly to the mortgagee, the IRS would have a strong case that in substance, the buyer assumed the loan, and there was no real "wraparound."

Elective Method

The installment method of accounting is elective with the taxpayer, in cases where it is permitted. In order to "elect out" of installment method treatment of deferred payments, you report the full gain on Schedule D (personal use property) or Form 4797 (for most rental property) and do not file Form 6252. Attach the main form to the tax return filed for the year of sale. If this is not done, the taxpayer will be deemed to have elected the installment method.

Electing Out of the Installment Method

What happens if you elect out of the installment method? Theoretically, two other approaches are possible: "closed" and "open transactions."

Trap

Be aware that the IRS generally frowns severely on the open transaction method and can be expected to challenge its use in most cases.

Closed Transaction Method

Under the closed transaction method, the buyer's notes or other evidences of debt are treated as though they were cash (i.e.,

taken into account at fair market value in determining the
amount of gain recognized in the year of sale).

Example.   Mrs. Smith sells property which has an adjusted basis
of $100,000, receiving $40,000 cash down and a note from her
buyer in the face amount of $260,000, payable in four annual
installments of $65,000, with interest at the rate of 9 percent per
annum. The note has "adequate stated interest," so the imputed
interest rules discussed above are inapplicable. Nevertheless,
because the buyer is in a somewhat precarious financial condition and his equity in the property is minimal, Mrs. Smith con-
cludes that the fair market value of the note is only $200,000.
This conclusion is supported by the fact that Mrs. Smith was
offered only $200,000 when she tried to assign the note to a bank.
   If Mrs. Smith elects out of the installment method, the gain
recognized in the year of sale will be $140,000 ($40,000 cash,
plus $200,000 fair market value of the note, less $100,000 basis).
Her basis in the note will be $200,000. Assuming that the note is
paid when due, Mrs. Smith will report an additional gain of
$60,000 over the period that the payments are made.
   The exact time that income is recognized is not entirely clear
from the law, regulations, rulings, or case law. Some cases support the view that gain will be recognized only after Mrs. Smith
receives principal payments aggregating $200,000. Other cases,
however, require Mrs. Smith to prorate her $200,000 basis in the
note over the four installment payments and report the $60,000
total gain anticipated in four annual installments of $15,000 each.

Tip

Taxpayers will usually prefer the first approach, after actually
receiving principal payments up to the note's basis, since it
defers payment of tax on the remaining gain for the longest possible period.

Open Transaction Method

The open transaction method would allow Mrs. Smith to defer
reporting any gain until the total payments she received equaled
her basis in the property. If the open transaction method were

allowed, Mrs. Smith would treat the down payment and $60,000 of the first principal payment on the note as nontaxable recoveries of investment or basis. The remaining $5000 paid with the first installment, and all of the next three installment payments, would be treated as gain from the sale of property (usually capital gain). Interest received would also be taxed, as ordinary income.

Under the regulations, the open transaction method is limited to "rare and extraordinary cases" where it is impossible to value the consideration received. If these regulations are followed literally, the facts that the note has a value less than face or that the buyer's credit standing is highly unfavorable would not permit use of the open method. In most cases, the method would be allowed only where it is almost impossible to forecast the amount of payments to be made, as in situations where land is sold that may contain mineral deposits, and the price is dependent on the amount or value of minerals extracted for a limited period of time.

When the Installment Method Is Not Available

Over the years, Congress has enacted many rules restricting the availability of the installment method. When it is not available, the IRS will usually insist that taxpayers employ the closed transaction approach, but some rather daring individuals may attempt to make use of the open transaction alternative.

The installment method cannot be used in the following circumstances:

1. Sales of actively traded securities
2. Recapture of depreciation under Section 1245 or 1250 of the Code (which is treated as ordinary income)
3. Property which generates ordinary income to the seller rather than capital gain, because he or she is considered to be a "dealer" in that type of property
4. Sales where the consideration received consists of an obligation that is actually a readily marketable security, such as a corporate bond issued by a company which is registered for trading with the SEC

Sale to a Related Person

There are several other cases where use of the installment method is restricted or partially disallowed. If a taxpayer sells property to a related person (as defined below) in a transaction that qualifies for installment reporting, but the related person, within 2 years, resells the property, the receipt of payments by the related person are usually deemed collections by the original seller, to a certain extent.

Example.   Mr. Murphy sells Blackacre to his daughter, Jane, for a total price of $300,000, payable $30,000 down and the balance over a 25-year period. His basis in Blackacre is $100,000, so his taxable gain, if all payments are to be received, is $200,000.

After 1 year, Jane resells Blackacre to Jones, an unrelated person, for $330,000, payable in cash. She continues to make payments on the note to her father and invests the proceeds from the sale of Blackacre in various securities and bank accounts. Although Mr. Murphy receives no proceeds from Jane's sale, the related party resale rule may require him to treat the amount of $300,000, less the small portion of principal paid by Jane in the first year, as a receipt from his sale to Jane, thereby accelerating his tax liability.

Exceptions to the Related Party Rule

The "related party resale rule" has many exceptions, however. For example, it does not generally apply where the related party's disposition is an involuntary conversion (such as a condemnation or sale under threat of condemnation), a tax-deferred exchange, or to second dispositions made after the death of the original seller or the original buyer. The law also contains an exception where the seller and buyer can establish, to the satisfaction of the IRS, that there was no significant tax avoidance purpose in either the first sale or the second disposition.

On the other hand, the 2-year period that normally cuts off application of the related party rule won't protect an installment sale if the related-party buyer engages in a transaction within the 2-year period that leaves him or her with a substantially diminished risk of gain or loss from continued ownership. Options to buy or sell property, which are likely to be exercised, are typical cases where risks of ownership are diminished.

Transfers of Installment Obligations

If the seller of property who receives an installment obligation disposes of the obligation before receiving all payments, any remaining gain is accelerated. Where the disposition is a sale, the seller reports gain equal to the amount received on the disposition of the note, over his or her unrecovered basis in the note.

Example. Mrs. Brown sold property, in which her adjusted basis was $100,000, for a $300,000 stated price, payable $50,000 down and the balance in a note payable over a 30-year term. After 5 years, the balance due under the note was reduced to $294,000. Mrs. Brown then sold the note to an unrelated party for $275,000. The excess of the amount she received over her remaining basis in the note is taxable as gain. This excess would be $275,000 less one-third of $294,000, or $98,000, which is, $177,000.

Trap

A real trap exists if the seller disposes of the note by way of gift. In this case, the gain is reported based on the fair market value of the note at the time of the gift, over the adjusted basis in the note. The seller is thus taxed as if he or she had made a sale of the note and then gave away the proceeds to his or her child or other beneficiary.

For example, assume, in the prior example, that Mrs. Jones did not sell the note, but gave it to her son, Sam, as a wedding present. Mrs. Jones must recognize gain equal to the fair market value of the note, $275,000, over her remaining basis in it, $98,000.

Actually, in cases like this, Mrs. Jones would have a burden of proving that the fair market value of the installment obligation is less than its face amount. If she cannot do this, the IRS is likely to calculate the realized gain as the entire amount of gain anticipated when the property is sold, less amounts on which tax was paid prior to the gift.

Tip

The only common exceptions to the acceleration rule in this context are when the transfer occurs by reason of the seller's death or in connection with a property settlement incident to a divorce. In the first situation, gain is not accelerated but follows the obligation to whomever properly receives it under the terms of the seller's estate plan or applicable state law.

For example, assume, in the prior example, that Mrs. Jones died instead of either selling or giving away the note. Her will left her entire estate to her son, Sam, after completion of probate administration. Mrs. Jones is not subject to tax on the deferred gain. However, her estate will be taxable on any installments of principal that it collects, and her son will be subject to tax on installments of principal that he collects following the closure of the estate. The installment obligation does not get the benefit of a stepped-up basis at Mrs. Jones' death. The note will also be subject to estate tax. However, Mrs. Jones' son may take a deduction for the estate tax paid on the note when he collects it from the debtor. The deduction is allocated, pro rata, to the principal installments received.

Bequests

A useful planning device in this context, where an individual intends to make gifts to charity by his or her will or revocable trust, is to specifically bequeath any installment obligations to the charitable beneficiary. The charity won't be subject to tax, ordinarily, when it collects the installments, and no "imputed" income will be charged to any of the other beneficiaries.

Example. Mr. Jones, a single individual who has been informed that he is terminally ill, owns an installment obligation with a principal amount of $200,000, of which $150,000 will constitute gain. His other assets include securities with a basis to him of $200,000 and a fair market value of $500,000. He intends to leave approximately $200,000 to charity and the balance of his estate to his sister, Susan. Good tax planning in this case would call for Mr. Jones to change his will so that the installment note, whatever it may be worth at the time of his death, is left directly to the charity, and Susan gets the other assets. By doing this, Susan will save a substantial amount of income tax compared to the result that would occur if the note and the other assets were left pro rata to the charity and Susan.

Poor Tax Planning

Even in a postdeath situation, there can be a trap in the treatment of installment obligations.

Assume that, in the prior example, Mr. Jones instead left a pecuniary amount of $200,000 to the charity, and the residue of his estate to Susan. His will authorizes his executor to satisfy the gift to charity with either cash or other assets whose fair market value is $200,000. The executor distributes the note to the charity in satisfaction of the monetary legacy. On these facts, the estate realizes a taxable gain of approximately $150,000 when it distributes the note to the charity, and the tax on this gain (approximately $50,000) directly reduces the net value distributable to Susan. This is, to put it mildly, terrible tax planning.

Pledges as Dispositions

In the past, the "acceleration rule" for installment obligations could be avoided by borrowing against the obligation and pledging it as collateral instead of selling the note. However, since 1988, this has not been possible. Today, the proceeds of any loan for which an installment obligation is pledged to secure repayment are treated as proceeds of sale, and deferred gain will be triggered.

Tip

The rule can be avoided only by borrowing on an unsecured

basis or using other assets as collateral. The former course will often be unattractive since most lenders are more willing to loan substantial sums only if acceptable security is posted. The latter course may not be available as a practical matter, due to the seller's lack of resources.

Recharacterization of Payments

If property is sold for an installment obligation such as a long-term note, and the obligation is either interest-free or does not carry an "adequate" interest rate, some or all of the payments received are recharacterized as interest, which is taxable as ordinary income rather than capital gain to the seller and which is often deductible by the buyer, instead of comprising a portion of his or her cost for the property.

This problem has little current importance. The tax law expressly states that a rate of 9 percent, compounded semiannually, is considered to be adequate, except in cases where the total amount financed by the seller exceeds $2.8 million, indexed annually for inflation.

Furthermore, as a result of the current low-interest rate environment, the IRS considers interest rates as low as 6% to be adequate. Note, however, that this "applicable federal rate" is changed monthly, and the rate for the month of sale must be determined before deciding what interest rate should be stated in the buyer's debt instruments.

Interest on Deferred Tax

If you are fortunate enough to take back, through sales of property made in 1 year, more than $5 million in installment paper, you will have the dubious privilege of paying an "interest charge" on the amount of tax that you defer with respect to the portion of the buyer's indebtedness in excess of $5 million. Happily, this problem affects few taxpayers, so those involved will have to consult professional advisors.

Repossession of Property

If a seller is forced to repossess property after a buyer's default, special rules govern the calculation of gain or loss flowing from the repossession. In general, the seller must recognize gain equal to the *lesser* of the cash received prior to the repossession or the total gain realized on the property.

Example 1. Jones sells a parcel of real property, in which her basis was $80,000, for a stated sum of $200,000, of which $25,000 was paid at closing and an additional $175,000 would be paid in seven annual installments, together with interest on the unpaid balance. After receiving one payment on the note, the buyer defaults, and Jones reacquires the property through a trustee's or foreclosure sale. In this situation, Jones received a total of $50,000 in cash but, prior to reacquisition, had only reported $30,000 as gain (treating $20,000 as return of capital). By virtue of the reacquisition, Jones must report the $20,000 previously collected as return of capital as additional gain in the year of reacquisition, reduced, however, by any expenses incurred in the reacquisition process. Ignoring these items, Jones' basis in the reacquired property will be $80,000, the same basis as she had prior to the sale.

Example 2. The facts are the same as in example 1, except that Jones' basis in the property was $160,000 instead of $80,000. On these facts, Jones would have reported only $10,000 in gain on the installment method. Since her total gain ($40,000) to be realized if all payments had been timely made exceeded the cash she received from the buyer, her gain on reacquisition is limited to $30,000; $10,000 of her receipts continues to be treated as recovery of capital. Jones' basis for the property following reacquisition will be $150,000.

Installment Sales as Tax Deferral Devices

As noted at the beginning of this chapter, the installment method of accounting is not considered by your authors to be the ideal method of selling property. Gain is only deferred, not eliminated, as may be the case in a tax-deferred exchanges if exchanged property is held until the death of the seller (or the first to die of a married couple). Further, as evidenced by this chapter, the rules are complex and contain traps for the unwary.

If you opt to use the installment method of accounting, you would be wise to consult with an experienced accountant or CPA at the outset.

10
Tax-Free Exchanges

Ever since the elimination of a lower capital gains tax rate, tax-free exchanges have been growing in popularity. Real estate investors see, in the tax-free exchange, an opportunity to dispose of an unwanted property (presumably one that has appreciated in value and been depreciated to a lower basis) and at the same time avoid for the moment paying tax on the gain.

"Tax Free"

In one sense, the term "tax-free exchange" is a misnomer because technically tax is deferred not eliminated when a proper exchange occurs. However, under current law, deferral can turn into forgiveness if the exchanger dies before converting to cash or other consideration. The exchanger's heirs take the property at a new, or (usually) "stepped-up" basis. This is true even if no estate tax is paid, as when the property transfers to the exchanger's surviving spouse. For this reason, tax-free exchanges are extremely important and valuable techniques.

Challenges to Tax-Free Exchanges

Compared to other areas, tax-free exchanges have survived successive waves of tax reform quite well. Although Congress did enact a few restrictions—such as forbidding the exchange of partnership interests from qualifying for tax-free treatment—the restrictions are often rather easy to plan around if people know what they are doing and are aware of the legal requirements.

Moreover, IRS regulations and rulings in this area are, in general, structured to facilitate, rather than hamper, individuals who want to structure exchanges.

Fundamentals of Tax-Free Exchanges

The law permits—indeed requires—property that is "used in a trade or business or for the production of income," when exchanged for real estate that is "of like kind" to be treated tax-free. The IRS regulations and applicable case law are remarkably liberal in defining the "like kind" principle, permitting almost any real estate to be considered "like kind" to any other real estate. Note, however, that there is legislation pending in Congress that could change this to a much stricter interpretation.

Tip

The IRS regulations expressly sanction the exchange of an improved lot in an city for vacant land or a farm located in the country. They also provide that leasehold interests for a term in excess of 30 years and "fee titles" to real estate are of like kind.

Disallowing Losses

Technically, Section 1031, which contains most of the important rules relating to real property, is not elective: It disallows losses just as much as it permits deferral of tax on gains. However, anyone who has an unrealized loss on property will generally be able to sell it to one person and reinvest the proceeds (or other funds) in property purchased from another. Such transactions are *not* qualifying exchanges and, therefore, the loss on the sale may be fully recognized. As a practical matter, therefore, Section 1031 will almost never apply to disallow losses on the disposition of real property.

Consequences of a 1031 Exchange

When Section 1031 applies, the consequence is that the replacement property has an initial (unadjusted) basis equal to the basis in the old property, increased, however, by any additional cash paid, or debt assumed, by the exchanger.

Example. Jones owns Blackacre, which has an adjusted basis of $60,000 and a fair market value of $200,000. He exchanges it for Whiteacre, a like kind property, with a value of $250,000. Because of the difference in equities, Jones either pays an extra $50,000 in cash or signs a note to Whiteacre's owner. In either case, Whiteacre's basis will initially be $110,000, the original basis plus $50,000 cash or note "boot" paid.

Boot

On the other hand, when boot is received, rather than given, the boot received is usually fully taxable, unless the value of the boot exceeds all of the appreciation in the property exchanged out.

Example. In the prior example, assume that the value of Whiteacre was only $180,000 rather than $250,000. Therefore, Jones would be entitled to receive, rather than give, boot to the tune of $20,000. If it is received in cash, it will be fully taxable. If it takes the form of a note, Jones will usually be taxed, in full, on it since principal payments are received (see discussion in Chapter 9 regarding the installment method of accounting).

Trap

Boot is a four-letter word when it comes to exchanges. Many experts in the field spend a great deal of time structuring exchanges so that there is no boot. The reason, of course, is that the boot is fully taxable and not transferable. It is important to understand, however, that taking or giving boot does not disqualify the transaction as an exchange. It only means that the boot portion becomes taxed.

Treatment of Debt

Where the property exchanged out of is subject to debts that the acquiring party assumes, or to which he or she takes subject, the amount of the debt so assumed or taken is usually considered the equivalent of cash and is thus taxable.

Example. In the first illustration, assume that Blackacre was subject to a mortgage of $30,000, which is assumed as part of the transaction, and that Whiteacre, worth $220,000, is acquired "free and clear." Jones' realized gain in this situation is $150,000—the value of Whiteacre received, plus the $30,000 assumption of debt, less his cost basis of $100,000. His gain is recognized (i.e., not subject to tax-free treatment) to the extent of $30,000. The balance of his gain is not recognized. His basis in Whiteacre will be the same as his old basis in Blackacre—$100,000 (increased by the costs and expenses of effecting the exchange paid by Jones).

Debt Relief

However, the income tax regulations prescribe a very important exception to the rule that assumption of debt is treated as cash received. Debt relief, in the form of assumptions of debt on the old property, may be offset by debt incurred on the new property. Any excess of new debt incurred over old debt assumed is added to the basis of the replacement property.

Tip

The general rule is that to fully defer gain on an exchange of properties, the exchanger must both (1) have a cost for the new property that is at least equal to the value of the old property and (2) take on at least as much debt in connection with the acquisition of the new property as he is relieved from by reason of disposing of the old property.

Deferred versus Nondeferred Gain

Example 1. Jones owns Blackacre, which has a basis of $130,000, a fair market value (before deducting encumbrances) of $300,000, and is subject to $100,000 of debt. He exchanges

Blackacre for Whiteacre, which has a value of $350,000 and is subject to $150,000 of debt. Jones uses the $200,000 net equity in Blackacre as a "down payment" on Whiteacre. Although Jones has realized a gain of $170,000, none of his gain is recognized (i.e., subject to current tax). His $170,000 of deferred gain is preserved because Whiteacre, in his hands, will have a tax basis of only $180,000, though its fair market value is $350,000.

Example 2. The facts are the same as in prior example, except that Whiteacre has a value of $200,000 and is not encumbered by any debt. In this situation, the $100,000 debt relief from exchanging out of Blackacre is considered like cash received on sale of Blackacre. Gain is realized to the extent of the value of this debt relief. Thus, although Jones gets no cash out of the exchange, he incurs liability for tax on a gain of $100,000. His basis in Whiteacre will be $130,000, $70,000 less than its fair market value. This is because $70,000 of his total gain has not yet been recognized.

Treatment of Consideration

The regulations permit consideration given, in the form of assumption of liabilities, to be offset against consideration received in the form of debt relief, and they permit consideration given in the form of cash or other property to be offset against consideration received in the form of debt relief. However, regulations prohibit a taxpayer from offsetting consideration received in the form of cash by consideration given in the form of assumption of liabilities.

Example. Smith owns Greenacre, with a basis of $210,000 and a current value of $400,000, which is free and clear. She exchanges it for Redacre, owned by Evans. Redacre has a current value of $450,000 but is subject to an existing loan of $100,000. To "balance equities," Evans pays Smith $50,000.

According to the IRS regulations, Smith must pay tax on the $50,000 cash received, even though she assumes $100,000 in debt. Her basis for Redacre will be $310,000, reflecting the fact that only $50,000 of the $190,000 appreciation in the value of Greenacre was subjected to tax, leaving $140,000 of deferred gain. (Redacre's basis in Smith's hands is $140,000 less than its current fair market value.)

Unusual Exchanges

Section 1031 applies only to exchanges of real estate for real estate and tangible personal property for other tangible personal property. It does not apply when either the property given up or the property received is an intangible asset, notably, stocks, bonds and, since 1986, partnership interests. However, Section 1031 does apply to exchanges of fractional interests in real property, such as undivided tenancy-in-common interests.

Stock Exchanges

Under other provisions of the tax law, however, certain exchanges of property for stocks can be tax-free. Likewise, in most cases, assets distributed upon the dissolution and liquidation of a partnership are also received free of tax. Hence, it appears possible to "escape" the rule that partnership interests are not exchangeable free of tax through proper structuring of transactions.

Example.   Smith, Jones, and Brown are partners in the S-B-J partnership, which owns two parcels of real estate. Brown wants to leave the partnership, receive the value of her capital account, and join a different partnership, whose partners are now Evans, Green, and Hughes. Hughes, in turn, wants to join the S-B-J partnership. At one time, Brown and Hughes could simply exchange their partnership interests, and, subject to any debt relief rules, have little or no taxable gain on the exchange. Since 1986, this has not been possible.

It remains possible, however, to accomplish the results in other ways. For example, it may be possible for the two partnerships to dissolve, so that the former partners hold their interests in the partnership property as tenants in common rather than as partners. Brown and Hughes could then exchange their respective tenancy-in-common interests. Or, conceivably, the partnerships could distribute one of their properties to Brown and one to Hughes. Brown could then contribute the property she received from the S-B-J partnership to the E-G-H partnership, and Hughes could then contribute the property he received from the E-G-H partnership to the S-B-J partnership. At a later time, the two partnerships could make a tax-free exchange of properties.

The techniques outlined above, and numerous possible variations, are controversial and have not been directly blessed by any court decisions or IRS rulings, although there are favorable decisions in analogous areas. Hence, caution should be exercised in structuring any transaction involving partnership interests or former partnership interests, and professional advice would be extremely valuable.

Three-Legged Exchanges

One of the biggest problems confronting prospective exchanges used to be that Mr. Jones might want to make an exchange, and Mrs. Smith might want to buy Mr. Jones' property, but Mrs. Smith has no property that Mr. Jones wants to acquire. The solution to this problem was the "three-legged" or "three-cornered" exchange—typically involving cases where Smith would purchase property designated by Jones and then convey it to Jones in exchange for the property she wanted to buy.

Three-cornered exchanges have become very common. There is a great deal of favorable case law in this area. For example, Mrs. Smith can actually designate the property she wants Mr. Jones to take; she can even arrange to have a straw party or nominee purchase the property with short-term financing that she will pay off when she buys from the nominee; and she can lend Jones the funds to purchase the property in excess of the value of her original property that Jones will be acquiring. All of these variations are blessed by case law or IRS rulings. (When a case has been decided in favor of the taxpayer, however, the IRS contends that it is usually not bound to follow the decision and may seek to litigate the same issue before more than one court.)

Delayed Exchanges

Several years ago, a gentleman named Mr. Starker had a slightly different problem. He had located a buyer for his property, wanted to complete an exchange, but had not located suitable replacement property at the time that his buyer wanted to close. Mr. Starker and his tax advisors came up with the ingenious idea of a deferred exchange, a technique that is often called, today, by his name—a Starker exchange.

Mr. Starker's Exchange

Basically, Mr. Starker conveyed his property to the buyer, Crown Zellerbach Corporation, in exchange for its *promise* to purchase suitable replacement property or properties at a cost not in excess of the agreed value of Mr. Starker's property, at some time in the future and convey the title immediately to Mr. Starker. Crown also agreed to pay a "growth factor," effectively interest, on the amount of the deposit. The IRS objected to treating this transaction as an exchange, but the Court of Appeals for the Ninth Circuit (which covers states, generally, on the West Coast and the regions immediately east of the coast) held in his favor. The Court stressed that Mr. Starker intended to make an exchange and never intended to have an unrestricted right to the cash proceeds that Crown held for the time being. The Court also held, however, that the growth factor was not eligible for tax-free rollover, even if it was used to purchase property.

Limits on Delayed Exchanges

Soon afterward, Congress amended Section 1031 so as to expressly recognize, but limit, the ability to make deferred exchanges. Basically, Congress laid down two principal limitations: A taxpayer must *identify* his or her replacement property not more than 45 days following the date of closing on the relinquished property, and the replacement property must *close*—that is, its title must be transferred to the taxpayer—within 180 days after the date that he or she transfers the old property. Technically, the exchange must also be completed by the time that the taxpayer files his or her tax return for the year of sale, but this date can take into account extensions of time to file. Since nearly all taxpayers can secure an automatic filing extension until August 15, the filing date requirement does not usually have much importance.

The text of the law passed by Congress left a lot of unanswered questions. For example, what was meant by "identification?" Could a taxpayer "identify" more properties than he or she actually purchased? Could intermediaries be used in the deferred exchange context? Could interest be paid to people involved in deferred exchanges without transgressing the new law?

Most of these questions, and many others, are answered in a set of IRS regulations that was originally proposed in 1990 and made final in 1991. Basically, these are helpful and workable rules which allow taxpayers a lot of comfort and security in planning exchanges, with respect to tax consequences. However, they do draw a number of arbitrary lines, and it is very important that they not be crossed.

The Time Limit Rule

The regulations are presently silent on whether the period for identification or replacement is extended if the last day of the 45- or 180-day period falls on a Saturday, Sunday, or legal holiday. The IRS originally proposed a specific rule stating that the period would not so be extended but withdrew it after protests. However, it has announced that it will still not allow any additional "grace period."

The Identification Rule

To satisfy the identification rule, the regulations require that property be identified in a written statement that is signed by the seller, which must be transmitted to either the "buyer" or any other person involved in the exchange other than the taxpayer or a "disqualified person," which basically means a family member of the seller, a corporation or partnership in which

the seller has at least a 10 percent interest, or a person acting
as agent for the taxpayer. Transmission by hand delivery, mail,
and facsimile are all permitted. Intermediaries, escrow agents,
and title companies are all eligible recipients. Alternatively,
a written agreement signed by all parties to a proposed
exchange, and signed before the end of the identification
period, will suffice.

Other Considerations in a Starker Exchange

The replacement property must be unambiguously described in
the written document or agreement. A legal description, street
address, or distinguishable name are the only sufficient descrip-
tions for real property.

A controversial aspect of the regulations is that they narrowly
limit the scope of "alternative" designations of real estate. If the
seller is not sure, on the forty-fifth day, about the exact property
he or she wants to acquire, he or she can identify either (1) no
more than three replacement properties (regardless of how
many separate parcels he or she may be transferring out) or (2)
any number of properties as long as their fair market value does
not exceed 200 percent of the aggregate fair market value of the
property being given up.

Trap

If you try to identify more than the above number, you automatically fail the identification test, unless you actually acquire
replacement property before the end of the replacement period
or actually acquire replacement properties that were identified
and that represent 95 percent or more of the total fair market
value of all replacement properties.

Replacement Examples

Example.   Tom, the transferor in a proposed 1031 exchange,
identifies as replacement property "a 200-acre farm in Madison
County." This is *not* an acceptable identification of property.

Example. Tom identifies the property as "the 200-acre farm owned by George and Wilma Smith, in Madison County, Virginia." This probably *is* an acceptable identification.

Example. Tom identifies five possible replacement parcels in his notice to the escrow agent. Unless he actually acquires them, or their aggregate value is no more than 200 percent of the property he is planning to relinquish, the identification will not be adequate.

Revocation of Identified Property

The regulations permit an identification of a property to be revoked, but only within the 45-day period. This can be important if the three-property rule or the 200 percent rule would otherwise be violated. Revocation of an identification must be made in a signed written document, sent or delivered (including by fax) to the person who received the original identification.

Using the Three-Property Rule

Once property is properly identified, the taxpayer had better be certain that he or she acquires substantially the same property as identified (or one of the three parcels, if he or she uses the three-property rule). Minor changes in the property, or a reduction in only the amount of what was acquired from what was originally identified, are apparently permissible, but more substantive changes will again cause a forfeiture of the right to exchange treatment, unless a Court can be persuaded to hold the regulations invalid.

Trap

The regulations take a fairly strict approach here. For example, they say that if a 2-acre farm property was identified, but the taxpayer eventually acquires only the land underlying the barn on the property and the barn itself, there is a disqualifying difference in the "basic nature or character" of the identified and the acquired property, so the exchange transaction fails the requirements.

Property under Construction

Sometimes, the transferor will want to acquire property under construction in exchange for his or her existing property. This is permitted for buildings; however, only the cost of the property incurred through the date of acquisition by the transferor may be taken into account. Any costs incurred after the transferor takes title are not considered costs of replacement property, but rather costs of the construction services being undertaken by the original owner of the property. Personal property that is still being produced at the time of transfer does not count, to any extent, as replacement property.

Using an Agent or "Safe Harbor"

The regulations provide that where cash or other property is received by an "agent" of the transferor, the transferor is considered to have actual or constructive receipt of those funds, and thus he or she may be barred from exchange treatment. However, he or she can then create three specific safe harbors. As long as the transferor does not have the right to demand immediate cash from his or her transferee or an intermediary, the IRS won't assert the constructive receipt doctrine, provided that the parties strictly comply with one of the three permitted safe harbors which are:

1. Qualified trust
2. Qualified escrow accounts
3. Qualified intermediaries

The key to successfully using any of these techniques is to avoid drafting contractual terms that permit the transferor the right, without substantial restrictions or limitations, to receive cash prior to the earliest of the date that (1) all identified replacement property is acquired or (2) the 180-day replacement property expires. One exception, which will be narrowly applied, is that the documents can give the transferor the right to receive the cash being held if a "material and substantial contingency" occurs that relates to the deferred exchange is provided in writing and is beyond the control of the taxpayer and any other person except the owner of the replacement property. An example might be the failure of the owner to clear up title problems or building code violations prior to closing escrow.

Letter of Credit

You can also structure arrangements to guarantee the transferee's obligations to acquire replacement property with a letter of credit or third-party guarantee without running afoul of the constructive receipt rules.

Qualified Escrow

In a qualified escrow, an account is set up to hold the cash proceeds intended to be used for reinvestment. The escrow holder must apparently be a third party who is not the taxpayer or a disqualified person. The rights to receive cash or other property must be expressly limited in the manner stated in the second paragraph above. Similar rules apply to trusts, which are different from escrow accounts only in some legal respects not generally important to people doing actual deals.

Intermediaries

Intermediaries, sometimes called "facilitators," are probably the most common method for handling deferred exchanges. In a typical exchange using this approach, the seller transfers the right to receive his or her property to the intermediary, who then assigns his or her rights to the buyer of the seller's property in exchange for cash to be deposited to an account in the intermediary's name. The regulations specifically permit title to transfer directly from the seller to the ultimate buyer, without a deed that is recorded to and from the intermediary. The intermediary then uses this cash to purchase the right to the replacement property; again, direct deeds from the former owner to the seller are specifically authorized. Moreover, the transferor and the ultimate buyer can enter into a contract of sale so long as the rights to transfer are assigned to the intermediary before the sale actually closes.

Treatment of Interest

It is very important to note that although growth factors, effectively interest, may be paid to the seller, no withdrawals can be made until either replacement property is acquired or the 180-day period runs.

The tax-free exchange remains an important consideration for property owners who want to dispose of investment property yet do not want to pay a high tax on their capital gain at sale.

11

How to Reduce Property Taxes

Thus far we have been discussing federal income taxes. However, anyone who owns real estate also pays a separate tax on the property itself. In many states this tax is very high, in some cases even higher than state income or, occasionally, even higher than federal taxes.

Yet, while most people grumble about their property taxes, almost no one attempts to do anything about it, on an individual basis. (People have banded together to force overall reductions in property taxes led by "Proposition 13" advocates in California more than a decade ago. In this chapter, however, we're talking about one person and one property.)

This is unfortunate because real estate taxes can be challenged by an individual taxpayer, and the chances of getting them reduced are relatively good in many parts of the country. This is increasingly so because as local governments have become more hard pressed for funds in recent years, and have raised property taxes, they have also frequently cut back on staffing in the assessor's office, meaning that the chances of an error occurring on your particular property taxes probably have increased.

In short, you could be paying many hundreds of dollars each year unnecessarily in excess property taxes. In this chapter we'll look at how your property taxes are determined and what you can do to challenge them.

Special note: Unlike federal taxation, where the rules are the same throughout the country, the rules for property taxation vary state by state and even county by county or city by city within a state. This chapter provides a general overview, and readers should contact a local source such as an attorney or tax assessor for information on local procedures and methods.

How Property Taxes Are Levied

Property taxes pay for such things as schools, fire protection, libraries, welfare, and other items that are of a local or, in some cases, a statewide nature. In the old days (before Proposition 13 in California and other similar laws in about half the states), the procedure for collecting property taxes was a highly politicized process. It worked something like this:

Elected officials for local governments, school districts, fire districts, and so forth would look at their estimated costs for the upcoming year and determine just how much money they needed to operate. Let's say that for a particular county, Miller county, it was $130 million.

Officials knew that they must raise this much money from all sources including sales, property, and other taxes. In terms of other sources, for this chapter we'll ignore other income such as sales tax. We'll say that the amount needed, after all other sources were accounted for, was an even $100 million.

To raise this money, the governing bodies of Miller county would tax all real estate. The only question was how to split up the tax bill among the individual pieces of property.

Tip

An important concept to understand here is that most real property taxes are *ad valorem* taxes. That means that you are taxed "according to the value" of the property. The owner of a house worth $500,000 pays 5 times as much property tax on his or her property as does the owner of a house worth only $100,000.

Another point to remember is that property is divided up into "classes" or "types." Residential property is one class. Industrial is another. Commercial is yet another. In many states, each class is taxed at a separate rate, but in others the rate is the same for all types of property.

To save time and expedite matters, many government bodies would probably prefer to simply assess a lot tax—divide the total number of lots in the county into the tax needed and then assess each lot the same amount ($100 million into, say 20,000 lots yields $5000 per lot). This would be easy to calculate and to assess. However, here the owner of a $500,000 house would pay the same tax as the owner of a $100,000 house. This is a method that almost everyone would consider unfair and could result in rioting in the streets if implemented across the board.

Hence, counties impose the *ad valorem* tax. They have a department, the assessor's office, determine the value of each individual piece of property, distinct from all others. That means that your house will have a separate evaluation, as will everyone else's. Then an appropriate amount of tax is levied.

Evaluating properties for tax purposes is a long and tedious process and is an area in which you may well be able to challenge and win a reduction. We'll go into it in detail shortly, but first a bit more on how the rate of tax for each property is determined.

Trap

Lot taxes are, in fact, becoming increasingly popular in areas where state constitutional amendments (such as Proposition 13) have restricted the ability of governing bodies to raise property taxes in general. For example, in California today it is not uncommon to have a lot tax of, say, $150 per residential lot to provide additional funding for a fire or school district. In almost all cases, however, these lot taxes must be voted in by the people who will be paying them (often by a two-thirds majority). About the only way to avoid these taxes is to defeat them at the polls or to convince the tax collector that your property is of a class (for example, commercial not residential) not covered by the tax.

Evaluating Individual Properties

In all states the county assessor goes to each property and determines its market value. For example, the assessor might come to your house and determine its fair market value was $100,000. The tax you pay is a rate based on that amount of value.

However, there may be many taxing authorities that draw funds from your individual property tax. Fire districts, school districts, libraries, and so on, each may be able to levy a tax and each levy it at a different rate. The result could be an enormous and unwieldy hodge podge.

To help equal things out, most areas have a "board of equalization" which examines the different rates of the different taxing districts and then restructures them. Often this is done by resetting the "assessed value" at an amount different from true market value. For example, your home's true market value may be $100,000. However, at that value, given the rates of the different jurisdictions, too much money might be collected. Therefore, the assessed valuation for your property might be set at 50 percent (or some other percentage) of that, or $50,000, in order to balance out different tax rates.

However, this procedure can easily become politicized with unfortunate results. The problem occurs because people tend to protest valuations that are close to market value. For example, the assessor may say the true market value is $100,000. But, since you know you're going to be taxed on the value, you're going to want it to be as low as possible. You may feel that it's only worth $90,000.

In fact, most people automatically find fault with the valuation placed on their property by the assessor. When tax is based on the value, the natural tendency is to contend that whatever value is given it is too high. After all, as noted, the lower you can get the assessed value, the lower the tax.

Therefore, in many areas governing bodies have taken to evaluating property at only a fraction of its true value as a political expedient. For example, your property's true market value might indeed be $100,000. But, for tax purposes the assessed value might be only 25 percent of market value. Therefore, on your tax bill, often in large print, the assessed value would show up as only $25,000. When you, as a taxpayer, receive your valuation from the county, you'd see the $25,000, and if you weren't too knowledgeable about the process (and didn't read the fine print), might feel satisfied with the low amount and promptly forget about it. In point of fact, relatively few people challenge valuations when they are calculated as a very small percentage of true market value.

The Tax Rate

The technique of placing a much lower assessed valuation than market value, however, becomes a political tool because it is still offset by the tax rate. Remember, this is the rate by which all property of a given class is taxed. For example, let's say that the combined requirement of all the taxing districts (fire, school, library, etc.) is that they must receive $2500 in taxes from every residential property worth $100,000 in true market value. Therefore, the tax rate on the property, if it is valued at full market price, ought to be 0.025 (100,000 × 0.025 = $2500). (Normally, the tax rate is determined first, 0.025, and then applied to each property within a class. However, going at it backward as we're doing here makes a point. Please bear with us.)

However, the assessed valuation has been set at one-fourth of the true market value, or in this instance, $25,000. A tax rate of 0.025 will only yield $625, far less than the county needs to meet its financial obligations. Therefore, the county raises the tax rate, in our case, by a factor of 4 to 0.01. Now the numbers work ($25,000 × 0.01 = $2500).

Note how by adjusting the *assessed value* downward and the *tax rate* upward you can get the same amount of tax. There's a political advantage, however, in having lower assessed valuations and a higher tax rate.

It's a fact that almost all tax payers readily recognize a valuation figure (especially when it's only a percentage of true market value), but few tax payers have a clue as to what a tax rate involves. Therefore, the taxing authorities sometimes placate the populace with a low assessed valuation, yet get the taxes they need with a high rate. The government has gotten the money without producing a lot of protests from tax payers.

Since, as noted, in most states the governing body (sometimes at the state level) can set what percentage of market value the assessed value will be and since local authorities can set the tax rate, by clever manipulation many taxpayers can be kept in the dark about the real cost of property taxes for years. The only thing they know is the bill.

Trap

Most people pay their property taxes as part of their monthly mortgage payment. Thus, when the county increases the tax rate and the resulting taxes, it only shows up as one-twelfth the amount each month and then often not until the next year when the loan impounds are recalculated. The true impact, thus, is often missed by many residential owners.

Tying the Hands of Government

Regardless of the actual motives for Proposition 13 in California (and other similar constitutional amendments in other states), two things that it did were to (1) mandate that all property be assessed at full market value at the time of the assessment, either when the property was first built or whenever it changed hands, and (2) ensure that the tax rate not exceed a set amount, originally 1 percent, since increased somewhat by voters. (It's up to the state legislature to then apportion the taxes collected amongst the various taxing districts—schools, welfare, etc.)

Thus, with a law such as Proposition 13 on the books, the hands of the governing bodies are tied. They cannot manipulate the assessed valuation of properties as a percentage of market value, and they cannot manipulate the tax rate. Therefore, everyone, it is presumed, pays their fair share.

Unfortunately, that's not the way it turned out. Since, as noted, property can only be reevaluated under Proposition 13 when it is first built or when it changes hands, after over a decade, we have the circumstance where the owners of two identical houses sitting next to each other may pay widely different taxes. In one house, bought 10 years earlier and evaluated at $100,000, the tax may be roughly $1000 a year (1 percent of full market value). The other house, however, bought only last month and having the benefit of 10 years of price appreciation, is assessed at $300,000 and its tax (at 1 percent) is $3000. The inequity will continue to grow as longer-term property owners pay far less in taxes than newer property owners, presuming values continue to appreciate (something that's currently in serious doubt in California).

Challenging Your Property Taxes

Now that we've taken a brief overview of how real estate is taxed and some of the inequities, let's consider methods of reducing your tax load. There are essentially only two ways for you (in some states only the first remedy is available) as an individual to have the taxes on your property lowered:

1. Challenge the assessment at the time it's made and have it lowered resulting in a lower tax
2. Challenge the assessment after it has been entered into the rolls and seek an "abatement" or a refund of taxes paid

We'll consider each separately.

Challenging the Assessment at the Time It's Made

The assessment of your property's value is first made at the time it is built. Typically, the tax assessor, who is an appraiser hired by the county assessor's office, examines the property and considers the following:

1. The cost including type of construction
2. The value of comparable properties
3. Factors that affect your property specifically such as neighborhood location, easements, hook-ups to water and sewer (or lack of them), and so forth

132   Chapter Eleven

After these considerations, the assessor then comes up with a figure for the value of your property (which is usually mailed to you) and publicly announced in a tentative tax roll. You now have a period of time (set in stone for each county) in which to challenge the assessed valuation.

If you don't challenge the assessment, it is entered into a permanent tax roll and you will be taxed based on your assessed value at the tax rate (discussed earlier). You may, however, still be able to later make a challenge before a review board, if your county has one.

Trap

Time is of the essence. If you fail to challenge the assessed value within the time limits before the final tax roll is set, as noted, your only recourse may be a review board held by the county tax assessor's or tax collector's office. There are also set time limits for this review process. Miss them and you may not be able to challenge your property taxes until the next tax year.

Tip

Tax years are normally not calendar years. Typically the property tax year runs from July 1 to June 30. Properties which are reassessed are often posted on a tentative tax roll in June and you may have until September to challenge the assessed valuation. If you fail to challenge, your property will be placed on the permanent tax roll and taxes may be due in December and February or March. Appeals or reviews may be held at times the taxing authority decides upon.

The best time to challenge the assessment on your property, in our opinion, is at the time it is first made, either when you purchase the home or when it is first built. A friend of one of your authors recently built a home and went through this process.

The tax assessor came by several times during the building of the property and measured it for overall size. She also checked the value of comparable properties to determine neighborhood values. However, the actual finishing of the home was delayed and no notice of completion was filed. (Until a notice of completion is filed, the home is considered still in the building stage.)

Each time the assessor came by to make a final valuation determined in part on the basis of the quality of the inside finishing (quality of the cabinets, paneling, etc.), the owner said it wasn't finished and told her to come back at a later date. (The owner had obtained "temporary" inhabitation permission from the local building department.)

Tip

It's up to the tax assessor to evaluate your property by making a personal inspection. However, there is no requirement that you make the assessor's work easier. While most states require that you allow the assessor to see your property, the final inspection should be done after all work is finished and then, usually, at a time convenient for both of you.

After nearly 3 months of delaying, the tax assessor in frustration finally said, "I believe the house is finished, even if no notice of completion was filed. If you don't let me see the inside of the property, I'll just assume it's up to the highest standard of quality in the neighborhood and base the assessment on that." At this point, the owner let her in. After all, the house was indeed finished. (In theory, any assessment made without actually viewing the property—the interior of the home in this case—can be challenged. However, to continue to refuse entry would only establish the taxpayer as a "hard case" and probably result in animosity, and perhaps a higher assessment and even fine, from the taxing board.)

What was gained by the delaying tactic? About a quarter of a year without the property being assessed at full value. During that time it was valued at far less, basically just the value of the lot. It amounted to a savings of nearly $400.

Once inside, the assessor glanced around and then sat down at the dining room table to announce what she felt was the value of the finishings. The owner protested the assessment. For example, the assessor indicated that the kitchen cabinets were worth $5000. The owner, however, produced a bill of sale from a discount supplier clearly showing that they only cost $1200. Further, since the owner had installed them himself, the cost of installation was negligible.

The assessor was frustrated. She appraised the fixtures, ceiling fans, tile, and so forth at a cost of $7000. Again the owner produced receipts proving they had cost only a fraction of that amount. At this point, the assessor sat back and changed tactics. She said, "It really doesn't matter what they cost you. What counts is their value once they are placed in the house and I can base that on comparables—what similar houses with similar finishings cost."

At which time the owner said, "Perhaps. But, I will challenge your estimates before the county assessment board and I will bring in my receipts. I doubt that the committee, at a public forum, will dispute them."

She leaned forward and said, "Would you accept a $2500 valuation for the kitchen cabinets?"

The owner replied, "$2000."

She simply said, "Done."

It's important to understand what's being discussed here. We're not talking about something illegal. Rather, it's the fact that appraisal is always an imperfect science and is up to the judgment of the appraiser.

No appraiser will look forward to having her (or his) work challenged by a savvy owner in front of bosses (the assessment board). It makes the appraiser look bad and takes up valuable time in what is certainly a crowded board schedule. It is much better to compromise and many assessors will, in fact, negotiate value.

The rule here is simple. If you tell the appraiser you will challenge and if you appear to have the information to back up your challenge, you may be offered a compromise.

Tip

Our suggestion is that you negotiate in good faith and accept a reasonable compromise. This is to be preferred to stonewalling and insisting on making a challenge before the review board. To do the latter may not get you what you want. Remember, unless there is some obvious error (discussed shortly) in the assessor's valuation which she or he refuses to correct, the review board isn't going to quickly overturn the valuation. They, after all, aren't on your side. They're trying to get as much in taxes as possible, while avoiding gross inequities. Once you're in front of the board, they will want you to "prove" your valuation is more correct than the assessor's, and that can be hard to do.

Trap

Always be polite. Yes, you may disagree with the appraiser, but don't insult him or her. If you do, you risk an angry response in which you might get an overestimate of the value of your property and a "dare you" to challenge it. A good compromise is almost always preferable to a fight where your chances of winning are not certain.

As suggested, the best time to get the value lowered is before the appraiser for the assessor's office submits the assessment. Discussing it over the dining room table is ideal.

Unfortunately, in the real world this often may not be possible. If that's the case, you may want to call the assessor's office and make an appointment to go in and discuss your home's valuation with the appraiser.

If you cannot get satisfaction from the appraiser, you may want to go higher up in the assessor's office. Typically there are several levels within the assessor's office to which you can rise while challenging the valuation. Ultimately, however, it comes down to what the assessor puts into the final tax rolls. If you disagree, your own recourse is an appeal to the review board.

Appeals

If you wish to appeal your assessment, you must check with the country tax calendar to determine when the board will meet. Then you must file an appeal prior to that meeting and well within the time guidelines given.

Each county will have an appeals procedure and they vary enormously. One county, for example, may allow you to make a personal appearance and state your case from beginning to end, including the discussions you may have had early on with the assessor's office. As in a small claims court appearance (although this is not at the level of the courts), you will have a few minutes to present your case. To win you must present compelling reasons that your assessment is incorrect.

Another county, on the other hand, may refuse to allow you to make an appearance and may only consider written material you submit. Further, it may only consider materials that you previously presented to the assessor and may not be willing to consider any new information you may have to present. You will want to determine exactly what the procedures used by your county are and follow them closely.

Trap

Remember, if you fail to timely file your appeal, you will probably lose your chance to appeal for an entire year.

Usually, taxpayers appeal the assessed value of their property and not the tax rate (although if the rate combines various taxing districts, this may be challenged on the basis that its unequally applied). They dispute the assessment, which they want lowered permanently (that is, not just for 1 year). However, you may also appeal for a tax abatement. For example, a portion of your home may have been destroyed by fire. You wish to have your taxes temporarily lowered until the property can be rebuilt. If granted, this could result in an abatement in which the overall assessment may remain the same, but you will pay lower taxes (or have previously paid taxes refunded) for a period of time.

Preparing a Challenge

In order to win your challenge to the assessor or, later, your appeal to a review board for a change in assessment, you must usually be able to demonstrate that the assessment is somehow wrong. There are numerous ways it could be wrong. However, in order to determine errors, you must first be able to see how the assessment was made. Typically, the assessor's office will have a file (or a card) on your property and in the file will be the information used to make the valuation of the property as well as the conclusions drawn from the valuation. Your first step is to gain access to that file, copy it, and then study it. Most assessors will make this information available to you.

Trap

Don't think that the assessor's office will be on your side. Once the assessment has been made, it's up to you to prove that it's incorrect. The assessor's office will be attempting to prove that the assessment is correct and that your arguments are not valid.

Tip

The challenge and appeals process involves forms that must be filled out and timely filed. Be sure to follow the procedure to the letter. Check with your local tax collector or assessor's office for the correct forms to use and when they must be filed.

Once you have your property's assessment file, you can check out the information contained within it. You are looking for errors that the assessor might have made. Of course, if you're not an appraiser yourself, you may not readily recognize incorrect information. Therefore, it may benefit you to get a written appraisal of your property's value from a state licensed appraiser.

Tip

Appraisers in the past have belonged to various trade organizations such as the American Appraisal Association and have had designations such as MAI which indicate their competence to make appraisals. Recently, however, many states have begun licensing appraisers. Since the licensing process usually involves having the appraiser pass technical proficiency tests as well as demonstrating experience, it is a good indication of a qualified person. Further, if you later present the appraisal report to a review board, the fact that the appraiser was state licensed will not be lost on that group.

Trap

A full written appraisal may easily cost several hundred dollars, which may be more than the amount you hope to get your taxes reduced. Therefore, you may want to make your own informal appraisal yourself. If you're careful, you may be able to uncover errors that will do just as well in winning your case.

Armed with the assessor's file on your property and either your own good knowledge or a private written appraisal, you're ready to check for errors. Here are some areas to which you may want to pay particular attention:

Size. Typically the value of an improvement such as a house is given in so many dollars per square feet. For example, your house may be valued at $70 a square foot. If the assessor says you have 2000 square feet, but you know your house is only 1500 square feet, the difference in assessed valuation is enormous:

2000 ft² × $70 =	$140,000
1500 ft² × $70 =	−105,000
Difference	$ 35,000

Simply going to the assessor (or the review board if you don't get immediate good results) and presenting evidence of a much smaller house size should result in a lower assessed valuation and a significantly lower tax bill.

Similarly, your lot is valued on the basis of its size. If the size is listed as bigger than it really is, you may be able to easily challenge the assessed valuation.

Of course, some readers may be wondering how errors could be made in something as simple as size. Rest assured, they are frequently made. Houses are often irregularly shaped, as are lots. Getting an accurate measurement may mean taking the time to plot the lot and house on graph paper and then making accurate mathematical calculations. An assessor in a hurry could easily make an error here.

Inadequate Comparables. In addition to cost of construction, tax assessors base their valuations mainly on comparables. The file on your property should list the comparables used and their values.

Were the comparables recent or were they out of date? Have prices gone down in your neighborhood since the comparables were sold? If so, they may be inappropriate for use in an appraisal. You may be able to bring in other comparables (preferably a list of homes similar to yours sold within the last 6 months and available from real estate companies) that show values to be significantly less. Since comparables are the main basis for establishing value, challenging the comparables used by the assessor can be your quickest way to a reassessment of your property.

Description. Check to be sure that your property is accurately described in the assessor's file. Does it have as many bedrooms, bathrooms, fireplaces, garage spaces, and so forth as are listed? If the assessor says you have five bedrooms and you have only four, chances are your house is assessed too high.

Tip

The assessor will always describe the condition of your property in terms such as "excellent," "good," "fair," "poor." Your house may be described as being in a "good" condition. However, it may be a total wreck. The walls may have holes in the them, the floor may be termite ridden, the roof may leak, and so on. With photos and/or an independent appraisal or property inspection report, you can challenge the condition listed for your property. Lowering the condition should result in a lower assessment.

Trap

Conditions change. If you get your property's assessed value lowered because of poor condition, then go in and fix it up, you can expect the assessor at some point in the future to reevaluate and raise the assessment accordingly. However, in those states where properties are reassessed on a regular basis, that reassessment is often years in coming. Many states only reassess, for example, every 7 to 10 years. Good timing of your refurbishing could result in many years before a reassessment is made. (See comments later in this chapter regarding fixing up a property.)

Errors of Fact or Calculation. Don't assume that the assessor got all the figures correct. Check the math. It could be wrong. Also, don't assume the assessor used the right tax rate for your property. Remember, different classes of property (residential, commercial, industrial, etc.) may have different tax rates. Was the right tax rate used? The assessor's office can provide you with a list specifying the tax rate for different classes of property. Finally, was your property classified correctly? If it's a home, was it classified as single-family residential and not some other classification?

Exemptions.   The property tax code for most areas provides for exemptions. These are automatic reductions in the assessed valuation of your property, provided you qualify. The most common exemption, generally for only a part of the value, is for homeowners. Another is for religious property, which is normally totally exempt from taxation and kept off the tax rolls.

If you personally live in the property in question (as opposed to being a landlord and renting it out to someone else), you may qualify for a homeowner's exemption. Typically in order to get this, you must have resided in the home on a particular day of the year, usually in the early months of the year, February or March, and must file for the exemption before the cut-off which is typically sometime in June. Check with your local tax collector or assessor's office for the dates in your area.

An exemption works in this fashion. The exemption may be for, say $7000. Your property may have an assessed valuation of $50,000. When the exemption is applied, the assessed valuation is reduced to $43,000 and that's the amount on which the tax rate is applied.

Checking to see if there are exemptions in your area and if you qualify for any of them is a very worthwhile few minutes spent. Usually it can be done with a simple call.

Tip
___

Most jurisdictions have both an assessor's office and a tax collector's office. The assessor's office, as we've seen, places a value on the property, applies the tax rate, and determines the tax to be paid. The tax collector's office then has the job of collection. For this chapter we are mainly concerned with the functions of the assessor's office. If you fail to timely pay taxes, you can have penalties, liens, and even seizure of property result, all of which are handled by the tax collector's office. Check with an attorney if you have this problem.

Most jurisdictions have separate assessor and collector offices. However, in some areas they are combined. When seeking information on filing deadlines and forms to use, be sure to determine how the assessor function is handled in your area and *call the correct office.*

Technical Errors. You may also be able to successfully challenge your assessment on the basis of technical errors made by the assessor. For example, as noted earlier, it is almost always necessary for the assessor to personally visit the property to make a proper valuation. If you can demonstrate that the assessor did not make the prescribed visit, you can challenge the valuation. All that this may get you, however, is a new assessor's appraisal. But, in the meantime (which can be months), you may be paying tax on an older, lower valuation.

Another common technical error is for the assessor to fail to take into account factors that detract from the value of your property. For example, you may have an easement (the granting of a right to someone else) over your property that allows, say, garbage trucks to cut across your backyard on the way to a landfill. Obviously, this is a detracting feature and lowers the value of your property. If it wasn't properly taken into account, your property may be valued too high. Other factors to be considered are whether or not your house complies with building and safety regulations, whether you are in a flood plain or geologically unstable area, and so on.

Other technical errors include the assessor failing to give you required notice, failing to follow state procedures, valuating the wrong property (someone else's property was assessed and you were given the assessment), failure to assess your property by the cutoff date, etc.

If the assessor's office made any of these or other technical errors, you may have sufficient grounds, once you point them out, to have your assessed valuation reduced or at least to be given a tax abatement.

Reassessments Caused by Improvements

Thus far we've been discussing property that was either brand new or was being reassessed in the normal course of things. There is another time assessments occur, however, and that is when you improve your property.

Every time you improve your real estate, presumably, you

increase its value and you warrant a new valuation. Therefore, be on notice that you not only have to pay for any improvements but for taxes on them ever after. This often catches many people by surprise. For example, you may have always wanted a nice new deck off the side of your house. Finally, you decide to bite the bullet and build the deck. You get your permit, buy your lumber, and spend several weeks putting it up.

Then, a month or two later, you get a notice in the mail that the county assessor's office has increased the assessed value of your property because of the new deck. You bought it and, perhaps, built it. And now you'll pay taxes on it.

Tip

The question always arises of how the assessor's office learns of the improvement you've made? The answer is the permit you took out. Building and safety permits are regularly reported to the county assessor's office. As soon as a notice of completion or a "final" has been signed, the assessor's office evaluates the work and raises your assessed valuation.

Trap

To avoid being taxed, some people will avoid taking out a permit. In other words, they will do the work themselves, or hire it out, without benefit of building and safety department approval. This is being penny-wise and pound-foolish.

Even if the work is done "up to code," without building department inspection and approval, you have no way of showing that the work met commonly accepted standards. If there should be a fire, or if someone should be hurt on the work, you could be liable and your insurance might not pay off. This is especially the case with anything involving gas, electric, plumbing, or structure.

The best advice is get the permit, get it inspected, and then take your chances with the assessor. It's safer that way.

The problem with improvements, particularly small ones such as decks, fireplace additions, overhangs, and so on is that it really doesn't matter, to the assessor's office, how much you actually paid. For example, recently one of your authors put in a fireplace in a master bedroom, with a permit. The total cost for materials was around $900 and the author did the work himself.

However, the valuation for the assessment was $1500. Further, the appraiser from the assessor's office never even came by but instead made the appraisal on the basis of the type of addition done and the description from the building permit. (Note: In some states, for small improvements such as this, no visit to the property may be necessary.)

This presents a problem for the taxpayer. Do you quibble with the assessor's office about the difference between your cost and the assessed valuation, or do you let it pass?

Trap

Keep in mind that if you challenge the assessment of a small improvement, an assessor undoubtedly will come out and look at the improvement. Along the way the assessor may also notice other improvements, such as new carpeting, fresh paint, new fixtures and decide that your house needs an overall reevaluation upward because of its improved condition.

Our advice is to forget the little stuff, unless you're sure you can demonstrate a lower valuation. In the case of the fireplace, without question it added value to the property, in reality probably twice as much value as the assessor gave it. Hence, regardless of what it actually cost, challenging the assessment probably would not have resulted in a reduction and might even have resulted in an increase. On the other hand, particularly if you haven't recently made any other improvements, the condition of your property hasn't improved, and the value of the improvement you just made is doubtful in terms of increasing property value, a challenge may be in order.

When You Improve More Than Half the Value of the Property

This is a "Catch 22" situation. In many areas, if you improve more than about 50 percent of the value of the property or 50 percent of the total area of the property, it is considered a rebuilding rather than an improvement. The difference is noticeable in many ways. From the building and safety departments perspective, rebuilding more than 50 percent may mean that they will require you to bring the entire structure up to current building code standards. Less than 50 percent and often only the part that is being improved will need to be brought up to current code. (Some jurisdictions have a set minimum amount of money, say $10,000. If you spend more than that, you trigger the requirement that the building be brought up to code.)

Another result of rebuilding more than 50 percent may be the complete reassessment of the property. Less than half and only the improvement may be considered. More than half and the total property could be reassessed. The tax difference can be substantial.

In this brief chapter we've just skimmed the surface of what's involved in real property taxation and challenging your home's assessment. Further, chances are that if you decide to actually challenge your property taxes, because of the relatively small amounts of money involved, you'll be doing it yourself without the aid of an attorney. Therefore, you will do well to bone up as much as you can on the subject. An excellent place to learn more is, *The Homeowner's Property Tax Relief Kit,* by Lawrence and Vincent Czaplyski, McGraw-Hill, 1993.

12

Real Estate Tax Planning Strategies

There was a time not that long ago when buying investment real estate automatically gave the purchaser tax advantages. Annual losses, often mostly on paper due to depreciation, could be written off against the owner's regular income, providing tax shelter. At the time of sale, favorable capital gains treatment allowed the owner to keep more of the profit. And depreciation terms were shorter, allowing for quick write-off of the investment. In short, it used to be the best of times for owning real property.

Times change. More recently with "active/passive" rules placed into effect, writing off annual losses against the owner's ordinary income has become impossible, except with an exemption noted later. Capital gains treatment, until very recently, was not much of an advantage. And much longer depreciation periods were established.

All this, however, does not mean that real estate can provide no tax advantages or that it is a poor investment. Quite the contrary; many tax advantages remain. The difference, however, is that now things tend not to fall into place automatically. Rather, the buyer of real property must think ahead, all the way forward to the resale of the property, in order to ensure the most advantageous tax treatment. In other words, the smart buyer must carefully plan the tax consequences of selling at the time of purchase.

Time Line

In fact, one of the most useful tools a buyer can use is a "time line." Here, the buyer plans, tentatively, for the term of ownership. It begins with the purchase date and ends with the sale date. Of course, the sale date is arbitrary, but at least it's something toward which to aim. It helps the investor to think of the property as an immediate turn over or as a 3-year, a 5-year, or a long-term investment.

Typical Time Line

Purchase date	Ownership period	Anticipated sale date
June 1, 1993	————————————	December 31, 1998

Tip

The longer you own investment property, the more you will depreciate it and, as a consequence, the lower will be your basis. When it comes time to sell, the lower the basis, usually the greater the realized gain (see Fig. 12-1).

Buyers who wish to resell for cash, therefore, often look at shorter ownership periods. To exaggerate the point, if you hold property for 15 years, you will have depreciated the property more than half its original value. Yet, your 30-year mortgage will only be paid down about 15 percent—most of the initial mortgage payments go to interest, not principal. Thus your equity produced as a result of debt reduction will be small, but your lowered basis will produce a large realized gain. You will have lots of taxes to pay without a compensating big equity.

One answer is to sell early for cash. Or to hold for a long time and then do a tax-free trade (described in Chapter 10).

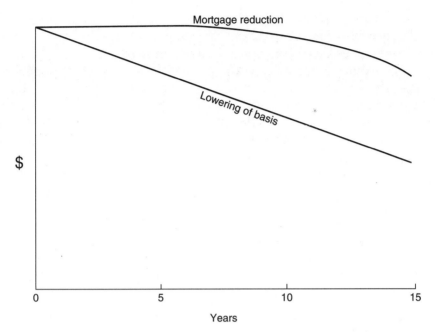

Years

Figure 12-1. During the first 15 years of ownership, basis may be lowered much faster than debt is reduced. As a result, assuming little price appreciation, upon sale taxable gain could easily be greater than equity.

Trap

Remember that how you finance your property does not affect the basis. Equity, however, is directly related to financing. One of the biggest traps owners fall into is confusing equity with realized gain.

Strategies When Purchasing

Here are some points to consider when purchasing an investment property.

Planning the Purchase According to Your Income

Perhaps the most important consideration we'll look into when purchasing a property with regard to taxation is how the purchase will affect your taxes. You may be able to lower your income taxes by paying special attention here.

For example, let's say your family's gross adjusted income is less than $100,000 a year. If it is, you should be able to take advantage of the up to $25,000 exclusion mentioned in Chapter 8. (If you earn between $100,000 and $150,000, you can take partial advantage.) In other words, it may be to your advantage to purchase a property that shows a loss each year so that you can deduct that loss from your current income. (See the discussion on tax shelters later in this chapter). In fact, if you can find a property or several properties with substantial loss, you can reduce your income by as much as the exclusion limit of $25,000. If you are in the 28 percent tax bracket, that amounts to a tax savings of $7000.

Trap

A tax saving is not usually worthwhile if you're spending money out of your pocket to achieve it. If, for example, your real estate loss is due to expenses that you have paid for in cash, being able to deduct them against current income for a tax savings does not constitute making a profit. In other words, if you spend $100 in cash and then save $28 in taxes, you are *not* coming out ahead.

On the other hand, if you can find property which breaks even on a cash basis, yet which loses money entirely due to depreciation (a paper loss), you may come out ahead. You will be spending zero, yet saving $28 out of every $100 in loss.

Trap

Be aware that when it comes time to sell, all that depreciation will have lowered your basis and increased your realized gain. As a result, you will probably end up paying taxes at the capital gains rate (currently 28 percent).

Thus, when you sell, you eliminate the benefit you achieved during each year of ownership. Of course, if you don't sell or if you do a tax-deferred exchange (see Chapter 10), this problem doesn't exist.

Trap

If you have a low income, beware of trying to purchase property to take advantage of the exclusion. You may not earn enough to see you through the difficulties of property ownership such as vacancies, repairs, and other problems.

Higher Incomes

On the other hand, a family earning more than $150,000 would not be able to write off a real estate loss in the current tax year because they would earn too much to fall within the $25,000 exclusion.

Tip

Higher-income families may want to consider properties with higher cash flows that break even for tax purposes. For example, a property with a positive cash flow of $5000, yet with a depreciation of $5000 will break even. For practical purposes, there will be no tax loss or gain to report in the current year.

Yet, the property will show a positive cash flow of $5000 (offset by the depreciation). This positive cash flow goes right into your pocket, yet you don't pay taxes on it, in the current year. For a family in a 39 percent tax bracket, this is a big bonus. You even get to keep some of the bonus when you sell because then gain will be taxed at the lower 28 percent capital gains tax rate.

Offset a Losing Property with a Winner

Another strategy is to buy a second property to offset one that you have. Under the passive activity rules, losses from one passive investment can offset gains in another. Thus, if you have a real estate investment that is showing a gain, you may want to buy another property that has a paper loss to offset it. Or, if you have one that shows a loss, you may want to consider a new property with positive cash flow to offset it.

The same holds true for a property that you sell for cash (no trade). In the year of the sale, you will undoubtedly have a substantial realized gain. However, if you purchase one or more other properties in the same year which show losses, at least part of the gain can be offset by the losses.

The idea is to offset properties to take advantage of the passive activity rule.

Time of Year

The tax advantages of purchasing at one time of year over another are minimal, but they do exist with regard to depreciation. Rental property (the house itself) is depreciated according to the month in which you buy. It doesn't matter if you buy on the first, the middle, or the end of the month. You still get 1 month's worth of depreciation. Thus, although it probably only amounts to a few dollars, if you buy at the end of the month, you get the full month's depreciation without actually having the expenses of ownership during that month.

With regard to personal property located at a rental, depreciation is automatically calculated on the basis of the "half-year" convention. This means that regardless of when you make the purchase, you are given a half year's worth of depreciation. Thus, purchasing in January means you will own the property for nearly a full year but only get the benefit of half a year's depreciation. On the other hand, buying in December means you will only own for a short time but still get half a year's worth of depreciation.

Of course, if you are able to expense the personal property entirely in the current year, you get a whole year's worth of write-off regardless of when you purchase the property.

Economics versus Tax Benefits

The above discussion should not, however, blind any investor to the importance of considering economics over tax advantages when purchasing.

One of the problems that the Tax Reform Act of 1986 addressed was the abuse of tax shelters. In prior eras real estate investments often were selected not so much for the economic viability as for their ability to shelter the tax payer's ordinary income. As a result, many investments that simply were not profitable were purchased. It's important to understand how these worked since the tax changes produced in 1993 may bring some of them back.

In the past a property might have a loss mainly on "paper" (due to depreciation) of $1000 a month. However, a real estate investor could then write off that paper loss against his or her ordinary income. Thus, the ordinary income (from wages or self-employment) that was taxable was reduced by $1000 a month.

A person in a high tax bracket was thus able to save a considerable amount on taxes by owning unprofitable real estate investments. Eventually when the property was sold, the investor, of course, had to pay taxes on the depreciated value (remember, depreciation lowers basis which upon sale usually results in higher realized gain). However, back then the tax was at a lower capital gains rate. Thus, real estate became an effective vehicle for lowering the tax rate of high-income taxpayers.

As a result, investors increasingly began purchasing real estate for its tax shelter benefit and less for its economic viability. This became widespread in the late 1970s and early 1980s in the form of limited partnerships where the investor often received little or no profit but substantial tax write-off benefits.

Of course, the Tax Reform Act of 1986 largely eliminated the tax shelter benefits of real estate by defining real property as a passive investment. With the exception of lower-income tax payers who could take advantage of the $25,000 exclusion (see Chapter 8), the write-off was effectively written off.

Tip

Every real estate investment should be able to stand on its own economically. In other words, either it should bring you a profit each month (positive cash flow), or you should be able to foresee making a profit upon sale that will more than cover any monthly net losses prior to sale. If it doesn't meet these criteria, why invest in the first place?

Trap
___

Most tax shelter advantages, as noted above, were eliminated by the 1986 Tax Reform Act.

Tip
___

Tax reform in 1993 offers a higher personal income tax bracket (as high as 39.6 percent, plus applicable state or local income taxes) than the capital gains rate (currently 28 percent, plus applicable state and local taxes). Thus, a real estate tax shelter is again possible. Those high-income taxpayers who invest in real estate and later sell for a profit will find their gain taxed at a much lower rate than their ordinary income. This promises to result in many high-income taxpayers again seeking real estate investments.

Taking Title

There are a variety of ways you can take title to property and there are some tax advantages and disadvantages to each. The basic methods are:

  Sole ownership (joint tenancy or community property)

  Partnership (limited or general partnership, tenancy in common)

  Corporation (Sub Chapter S corporation)

  Real estate investment trust, or REIT (stock purchase)

  We have already discussed the advantages and disadvantages of sole ownership throughout this book. That leaves the remaining methods.

Partnership

You can participate in a general partnership or a limited partnership or join with others as tenants in common when you take title to property.

  Forming a general partnership means that you can combine your money and your expertise with others for better purchasing power and control of your real estate investment. However, if you form a general partnership, you must file partneship returns, although the partnership itself does not have to pay taxes. Rather, it is a conduit to you for income and loss. However, the tax forms are somewhat cumbersome and failure to file can result in penalties.

In addition, you are liable for your partners' actions and, in some cases, their debts. As a result, many investors prefer a "limited" partnership. Here your participation is limited. Generally your liability in terms of economic loss is limited to the amount you invest. However, in a limited partnership, by definition you lose control. The general partner may run the real estate into the ground and you may have little recourse. Also, you may find your tax liability is substantially more than the amount you invest in the form of interest and penalties, particularly if there were deficiencies in the way the limited partnership was originally set up. And the general partner must still file partnership returns.

Trap

Limited partnerships were popular, as noted earlier, when real estate tax shelters were available. The limited partners entered into them mainly to lose money (on paper). Now that the tax shelters have been largely eliminated, these are no longer popular investment vehicles. Be very careful of investing in a real estate limited partnership today.

A tenancy in common is where you take title to the property with others without the right of survivorship. (Upon your death your interest in the property passes to your heirs and not to the remaining owners, as would be the case, for example, in a joint tenancy.) An advantage of this form of ownership is that no one needs to file a partnership tax return; each partner's share of income or loss is simply reported on his or her own Schedule E and on Form 8823. However, bear in mind that the IRS may say that you are a partnership in fact, unless the tenants in common engage in very little active management activities. The best case for *avoiding* partnership status is when property is "triple net leased," that is, the tenant occupies under a long-term lease and is responsible for all costs including taxes, insurance, and maintenance.

Corporation

Another way to own real estate is to form a corporation and then
have the corporation buy the property. The advantages here are
limited liability and the fact that real estate losses *within* the corporation may be written off, in some circumstances, against
other income from within the corporation. In other words, the
real estate can form a kind of corporate tax shelter.

The disadvantages are that you have double taxation (the corporation is taxed once and then you, as a stockholder, are taxed
on dividends you receive), it is costly to form and maintain a
corporation, federal and state security and tax laws are complex
and usually require an expensive CPA or tax attorney to handle,
it can be difficult to get property out of a corporation, and
financing property through a corporation can be difficult. (Most
lenders want an individual to be responsible for a mortgage.)

S Corporations.   Some of the problems are removed by using an
S corporation. These are simplified corporations which are run
much like partnerships. There is no double taxation, and the
profit as well as the tax shelter benefits flow through to the owners. And you can have as much as 100 percent of the S corporation's income derived from passive investments, such as real
estate. However, unlike the case with partnerships, debt incurred
by the corporation does not provide a "basis" to the stockholders
for the purpose of writing off losses.

Tip

If you already have a corporation, particularly an S corporation,
you may want to investigate the possibility of purchasing real
estate within it. While setting up an S corporation solely for the
purpose of buying real estate probably doesn't have enough
advantages, given the complexities involved, owning real estate
within an existing corporation set up for a different business
endeavor may.

Real Estate Investment Trusts

REITs set up to generate income or capital growth or both were
popular in the 1970s. They largely disappeared in the early 1980s

when limited partnerships were at their height. Recently they have returned.

Here essentially a corporation buys real estate and you purchase stock in the corporation. Profits are passed on as dividends, with no tax at the entity level. For the most part there is no pass through of losses.

REITs must meet numerous tests for qualification, including a minimum of 100 investors. Thus, they don't make sense as a vehicle for structuring a direct investment in property.

Strategies during Ownership

During ownership, there are a number of things that you want to do that will be advantageous to you from a tax perspective. Most of these have to do with how you handle costs. To maximize your tax advantages, during your term of ownership you should attempt to handle costs as described below.

Always First Attempt to Expense Costs

Expensing means that you deduct the costs during the current year. The biggest write-off you can get is to list the entire cost as an expense in the current year. If you qualify for a write-off against your ordinary income (the $25,000 passive income exclusion), the expense directly reduces the income on which you pay taxes.

Some items, such as interest and taxes, are always deductible in the current year. Other recurring expenses, such as insurance premiums, are likewise expensed. In some cases other items may be expensed as Section 179 costs. See Chapter 6 for details.

Tip

Don't forget your direct costs in managing the property. These include mileage to and from, costs of being there such as sleeping accommodations and meals, as well as phone calls and advertising. Normally these can all be expensed in the current year.

However, as noted in Chapter 6, there are many other items

which may or may not be expensed. A lot depends, for example, on whether the cost is a repair or an improvement. A repair generally can be expensed in the current year. An improvement must be depreciated.

Tip

If you're not sure, check with an accountant to see if your cost qualifies as an improvement or a repair. The tests are often in a gray area. Yet, if the item qualifies, expensing it can be a tax advantage.

Always Try to Depreciate Costs that Can't Be Expensed

If it turns out that you can't expense your cost in the current year, the next best thing is to depreciate it. (If cost is indeed an improvement, rather than a repair, you are stuck with depreciating it.) Most costs that can't be expensed can be depreciated.

Be sure to use the *shortest* permitted depreciation recovery period. The depreciable period for most items found in rental property, such as carpets, refrigerators, and appliances, etc., is 7 years. By depreciating the item you can use at least a portion of its cost to offset rental income in the current year. Also the shorter the term, the higher the annual depreciation.

If You Can't Expense or Depreciate It, Amortize It

Some items, such as some of the costs of refinancing, cannot be depreciated. Instead, they must be amortized over the life of the mortgage (see Chapter 6). While you may not be able to deduct these direct costs in the year incurred, you should be able to at least deduct them slowly while the mortgage is being paid back.

If You Can't Expense, Depreciate, or Amortize, Consider Adding It to the Basis

Generally speaking, any actual cost that can't be expensed in the current year or depreciated over its life or amortized over the loan period but is not specifically disallowed can usually be added to the basis. Adding to the basis will often result in reducing the gain you will realize on sale.

Adding to the basis is the last resort because you get no benefit at all in the current year. Your only tax benefit is when you sell down the road.

Trap

During ownership, the temptation to refinance in order to withdraw equity is ever present. There is nothing wrong with this. *Refinancing does not affect the tax status of the property.*

However, refinancing to withdraw money from the property reduces your equity. Yet, since your basis is unaffected, the gain you will receive upon sale continues to grow as the basis is reduced largely through depreciation. As noted elsewhere, you could end up with a small equity and large realized gain. In short, refinancing could mean that later on down the road you won't have enough equity to pay the taxes on the sale of the property.

Strategies When Selling

There are essentially only three options when you sell investment property. (Actually there are four if you consider retaining ownership and not selling at all as an option.) These are:

Sell for cash

Trade

Sell on an installment plan

Selling for Cash

Most owners want to sell for cash. (Of course, the buyer doesn't necessarily put up all cash. The buyer may get an 80 or 90 percent mortgage and put down only 20 or 10 percent. You, however, get all cash out of the sale.) The advantages are that you are once and for all through with the property and you know exactly where you stand at the end of the sale. Selling for cash is a nice, clean way of handling a deal. Unfortunately, when it comes to investment property today, it can be a tax disaster.

The problem with selling for cash is that all of your gain is recognized in the current year. (Remember, the gain realized is the difference between the adjusted basis and the net selling price.) At the current capital gains rate of 28 percent, that means that a substantial portion of the gain goes to taxes.

Cash Sale. Henry and Jane sold the rental home they had owned for 10 years for $200,000. They originally bought it for $120,000. The remaining balance on their original first mortgage was $97,000. They had refinanced once and had a second mortgage with a remaining balance of $45,000. The adjusted basis (they qualified for the $25,000 passive exemption and had depreciated it by roughly $4000 a year for 10 years—they used a shorter recovery period allowed when they made their purchase) was $80,000. The net sales price was $180,000. The cash out of the property (equity) was as follows:

Net sales price	$180,000
Less first mortgage	−97,000
Less second mortgage	−45,000
Equity	$38,000

The gain realized on the sale was:

Net sales price	$180,000
Less adjusted basis	−80,000
Gain realized on sale	$100,000

If the $100,000 of gain realized is taxed and Henry and Jane pay taxes at the 28 percent capital gains rate, their federal tax will be $28,000. That means that of their $38,000 in equity realized on the sale, $28,000 will go toward taxes.

Trap

The above calculation only takes into account federal income taxes. State taxes may likewise be due and, depending on the tax rate in their state, could use up the remaining $10,000 of equity realized on the sale. In other words, they could end up with nothing.

Tip

In the above calculation, Henry and Jane had reduced the basis by qualifying annually for the $25,000 passive income exemption. If they had *not* qualified for it, their annual loss on the property would have been carried forward and would have been applied toward the gain on sale, thus reducing it substantially. The amount carried forward for depreciation alone would have resulted in a $40,000 higher adjusted basis ($120,000) and a gain realized of only $60,000. This would have resulted in taxes of only $16,800 at the 28 percent capital gains rate. Other losses carried forward could have reduced this even more.

Trade

The above example should make it clear why selling for cash a piece of investment property that has been owned for any length of time and which qualified for the $25,000 exemption, makes poor sense. Much of the equity remaining in the property goes to taxes. It is for this reason that many savvy investors today would rather trade than sell.

Trading.   As explained in Chapter 10, a tax-deferred trade, if properly handled, results in no recognized gain. Rather the gain realized from one property is fully transferred to another property. It isn't overlooked or forgiven. The gain is simply deferred to the future at such time as the second (or subsequent property) is sold for cash.

Tip

One of the reasons that many people prefer not to trade is that they want to get cash out of their property. In a trade, any cash, or boot, taken out will normally be taxed.

However, this problem can often be overcome in one of two ways. Cash can be withdrawn from the first property *prior* to the trade by refinancing. Or cash can be withdrawn from the second property *after* the trade, again by refinancing.

While it's true that refinancing can cause an increase in monthly payments, this increased cost may be deductible in the current year (if the owner qualifies for the $25,000 passive income exemption). In any event, the increase in monthly payments caused by refinancing should be a small penalty to pay for being able to legally avoid paying the taxes due in full on a cash sale.

Using an Installment Sale

As explained in detail in Chapter 9, an installment sale involves carrying back some of the paper (mortgage) on the property being sold. The tax on the gain from the sale is recognized only as the mortgage is paid back according to a complex formula.

The advantage of the installment sale is that in future years you might be in a lower tax bracket. If that's the case, you will pay less tax on the income as you receive it.

Trap

Current tax rates move you up to the 28 percent capital gains bracket very quickly. (As of 1993, the marginal tax rate of 28 percent is achieved with $36,900 of taxable income in the case of married couples filing jointly; for singles it is at a taxable income of $22,100.) Thus, if you already are at or above the 28 percent tax bracket, you won't get any tax advantage by spreading the gain out over future years in an installment sale.

All-Purpose Strategies

Thus far we've been concerned with the time line—strategies to use when buying, owning, or selling a piece of real estate. Now we're going to consider some all-purpose strategies, those that can be used at any time.

Maximize Your Deductions by Paying Both Installments of Property Tax in First Year

Usually property tax on investment real estate may be paid in two separate installments, typically in December and in March. However, you may elect to pay the entire property tax on the first installment. By doing so, you increase your deduction for taxes in the current year.

Trap

Once you begin doing this, you must continue to pay both installments at the first installment date or else you'll end up with paying only half your annual taxes in a subsequent year.

Tip

This is an advantage primarily if you fall within the $25,000 passive income exemption. This allows you to apply the entire year's taxes on your rental real estate against rental income, presumably helping to produce an increased loss. If you do not fall within this exemption, however, there really is no benefit in paying your property taxes early since you'll just be carrying any loss forward until the property is sold.

Avoid Being Considered a "Dealer in Real Estate"

There are no hard-and-fast rules about who is a dealer in real estate and who simply purchases for investment. The danger of being classified a dealer for a particular parcel of property is that you may *not:*

Use Section 1031 tax-deferred exchanges

Do installment sales

Claim depreciation on the property pending its sale

Obviously, if you intend to take advantage of any of the three items noted above, you would not want to be considered a dealer for that property. A dealer is one who uses a real property as "stock in trade" and holds property for sale to customers in the ordinary course of a business. Most developer-builders are dealers in real estate with respect to property that they construct for the purpose of sale.

The best way to avoid dealership status is to engage in few sales in any one year, conduct whatever selling you do through brokers rather than extensive personal solicitation for bids, and use property for an extended period for rental purposes rather than just for sale. Unfortunately, there are no bright line tests for this question.

In 1992 the IRS issued new regulations for applying the passive activity rules to persons who might be considered dealers in real estate and would thus not generally be deemed to realize passive income from their sales [Section 1.469- 2(c)(2)(v)]. Under some restrictive conditions, offering property for sale won't be considered to take property out of the passive income category if sales promotion was less than 24 months in duration or there were both sales and rental activity for less than 25 percent of the time that the property was held for rental purposes as well.

In this chapter we have examined some of the strategies you may want to use when you purchase, hold, and sell investment property. Keep in mind that good tax planning can result in significant savings.

13
Record Keeping

There are two important reasons that you want to keep records:

1. If you own investment real estate or even just a personal residence, many products and services that you buy may be deductible or added to your basis. You need to keep records in order to remember what you bought.
2. If you deduct an item or add it to your basis, you may later be challenged by the IRS. The record that you keep is your proof that you bought the product or service and for what it was used.

In short, if you plan to deduct it, or add it to basis, keep a record. If you don't keep a record, forget about deducting it, now or later.

Trap

Some records are easier to keep than others. For example, when you buy or sell a property, you'll normally get a closing statement from the escrow company that handles the deal. It should detail every item that you paid for as part of the deal. Most people just naturally hang onto these closing statements.

However, it's a different story with other receipts. For example, a garbage disposer goes out in a rental unit you own. You go to the store and buy a new one along with additional parts and put it in yourself. Did you remember to keep the store receipt? What about a notation on the mileage driven to the store and the rental unit while fixing the broken disposer? What about a log of phone calls made to the tenant and to different stores before you found the right parts?

If you keep adequate records, you can justify all legal deductions. Without records, however, it's simply your word, or more often your faulty memory, to prove you paid the money.

What Is a Record?

A record is a receipt or an invoice for a product or service that you purchased. If you paid by check, your returned check should be attached to the receipt or invoice to show that you paid. If you paid by a credit card, the credit card slip should be attached. (Also, hang onto your credit card monthly statements, where the bill will appear, as well as your check to the credit card company showing that you paid.)

Your record or receipt must clearly state the following in order for it to suffice as documentation of the purchase:

1. *Name of vendor.* Often stores have register receipts that either fail to print the name of the vendor or the ink is so faded you can't read the name. Ask the store if it has an imprint it can stamp on an illegible receipt. In a worst case, have the clerk write out the store's name and sign the receipt.
2. *Date.* This is almost always included on register receipts. However, workpeople who prepare their own invoices often forget it. If you have someone come out to fix a fence on your rental home, be sure the invoice is dated.
3. *Amount.* It's hard to imagine an invoice or receipt not including this.
4. *Product or service you bought.* It's not enough to go to a hardware store and come out with a receipt that says you spent $5.33 on something. Was it a plumbing item? Was it electrical? Or was it a bunch of candy bars for the kids? The name of the product or the service performed must be spelled out.

If a receipt doesn't do that, have the clerk write it out and
sign it.

5. *The reason you bought it.*   You must show the business purpose
you had for the product or service. A good way to do this is to
turn over the receipt and write out the reason you bought it on
the back at the time of purchase. Be sure to list the location of
use if it's a rental property.

Tip

When it comes to receipts, the rule is do it now. Don't wait until
later. If you wait, you may forget.

Trap

A canceled check is often not enough. The check made out to an
individual, firm, or store really doesn't give all five items noted
above. The IRS could deny the deduction if the only record you
have is a check. However, a check stapled to an invoice or
receipt containing all five items listed above for a legal deduction is virtually undeniable.

Trap

Don't forget about returns. If you get to the rental property and
find that there's nothing wrong with the existing garbage disposer except that the tenant has clogged it up and you later
return the new garbage disposer, you can't deduct it.
Technically you should keep records of both the purchase and
the return. For practical purposes, however, more people simply
don't make the deduction on a returned item.

Logs

Some expenses do not produce receipts. These include phone
calls and mileage on your car. Usually the mileage to and from a
rental house or to and from a store to purchase a repair item is
deductible. The best way to keep track of it is with a log. This is
a book that you keep in the glove compartment of your car or
above your visor that you use to note all business trips you

make. A less desirable method would be to reconstruct trips you made from receipts you have. For example, if you have a receipt for a garbage disposer noted above, you will conclude that you had to go to the store to get it and then to the rental to put it in.

Similarly, if you plan to deduct a part of your phone cost, you should have a log showing the business calls you made. Ideally, you would have a separate business phone, but many investment property owners do not feel they can afford such a service. A log of business calls, later tallied against your detailed phone bill, should help. A typical mileage log might look like this:

Date	Destination	Business Purpose	Mileage Beg.	End	Business miles
3/24	Rover St. Prop	Check disposer	43,203	43,223	20
3/24	ABC Hrdwre	Buy disposer	43,223	43,233	10
3/24	Rover St. Prop	Install disposer	43,233	43,243	10
3/24	Home	From Rover	43,243	43,262	20

Trap

Keep in mind that travel expenses are not deductible unless the principal purpose of the trip is business related. In this regard, ownership of rental real property that produces income is considered a business. However, you cannot deduct expenses merely for looking at property that you may want to buy. If you start negotiations to buy but the deal falls through, there is a basis for deducting your costs as a business loss or expense. If you actually purchase the investment property, your looking expenses are added to basis.

Travel after Purchase

Once property is purchased, travel that is reasonably necessary and appropriate for maintaining it is deductible. However, don't assume that just because you buy a time-share in Tahiti, you will be able to write off all of your expenses of getting there. If the primary purpose of your trip is to take a vacation, in general, none of your travel expenses are deductible; however, costs that you can definitely associate with days of "business" activity can be deducted. If your primary purpose for making a trip is for business, including maintaining rental properties, your transportation costs are deductible if the trip is within the limits of the United States. Probably 50 percent of your subsistence costs (meals, lodging, and incidentals such as laundry) are deductible as well. If the trip takes you outside the country, however, the transportation costs must be allocated between business and pleasure, under complicated rules prescribed in the IRS regulations. Also, in all cases, you must keep and retain detailed records supporting the purpose of the trip, the validity of the expenses incurred, and the amount of the expenses.

Where to Keep Your Records

It is important that you keep your records organized and in a central location. Records that are left strewn about the house tend to get lost. An excellent method of handling this is to buy one of the many types of file folders that are available on the market. They come in paper, plastic, or as a hard filing box. Each time you get a receipt, simply stick it into the folder for the appropriate property. In this manner by year's end, you will have kept all of your receipts in one place.

Tip

Buy a separate folder for each property. Then, create files for each of the expense areas you will have. This way, at the end of the year, you will have all your receipts organized.

File Categories

Here's a fairly complete list of file areas to keep for a typical rental home:

Advertising	Auto and travel
Association dues	Check register and checks

City inspections	Painting and decorating
Clean-up/fix-up	Pest control
Electrical	Plumbing
Gardening	Pool
Insurance	Pool maintenance
Legal and professional fees	Repairs
Licenses and permits	Spa maintenance
Management fees	Taxes—real estate
Miscellaneous	Telephone
Mortgage interest (paid to banks, etc.)	Utilities
Other interest	

Records that You Will Want to Keep

Having noted the need for record keeping as well as how and where to keep records, let's finish this section with a list of the types of receipts, invoices, and so forth, that you will want to keep for an investment property (rental) versus a personal residence. (Remember, only some items for a personal residence are deductible or may be added to basis.)

Records to Keep for Tax Purposes

	Rental	Personal residence*	
Advertising receipts	X		
Association dues	X		
Auto and travel	X		
Casualty losses	X	X	
Check register and checks	X	X	
City inspections	X		
Clean-up/fix-up	X	X	(prior to selling)
Credit card statements	X	X	

Records to Keep for Tax Purposes *(Continued)*

	Rental	Personal residence*
Electrical improvements	X	X
Electrical repairs	X	
Garden maintenance	X	
Insurance premiums	X	
Invoices	X	X
Landscaping	X	X
Legal and professional fees	X	
Licenses and permits	X	
Loan amortization schedules	X	X
Loan payoffs	X	X
Loan statements	X	X
Management fees	X	
Mortgage interest	X	X
Painting and decorating	X	X (prior to selling)
Pest control	X	
Plumbing improvements	X	X
Plumbing repairs	X	
Pool improvements	X	X
Pool repairs	X	
Purchase orders	X	X
Repairs	X	
Room additions	X	X
Settlement statements (Property bought or sold during year)	X	X
Spa maintenance	X	
Tax bills	X	X
Taxes—real estate	X	X
Telephone expenses	X	
Utilities	X	

*You may want to save many items on the above list just to have a record of them in case of warranty or other problems.

14
Capital Gains and Losses

For almost 70 years, from the early days of the federal income tax until 1986, long-term capital gains were entitled to "preferential" treatment. At various times, the preference was an "alternative" tax at the rate of 20 percent, or a 50 or 60 percent deduction or, in some years, whichever approach provided the greatest benefit to the taxpayer. Of course, in order to qualify it was necessary to hold the property for a specific minimum period of time. The holding period necessary for favorable treatment was sometimes 6 months, sometimes 1 year. With the exception of "dealer" property, real estate generally qualified for capital gains benefits to the extent that gain had to be recognized and taxes paid at all.

In 1986, the benefits of long-term capital gain treatment were suddenly—one might say rudely—eliminated. There was, however, a minor exception. Under today's law, the maximum tax rate on a long-term capital gain is 28 percent, even though the rate on ordinary income can go as high as 39.6 percent. But this small differential is peanuts compared to what had long been the case.

Capital Losses

Even as capital gains were historically favored by the law, most capital losses were disfavored, and adverse treatment of these capital losses continues to be the rule today. The main "adverse" rule is that capital losses can only be deducted against capital gains, plus at most $3000 of ordinary income.

Tip

If an individual taxpayer has a capital loss in excess of $3000, he or she must carry it forward and offset it only against future capital gains, if any, or up to $3000 of ordinary income in the subsequent years.

Example.   In 1992, Jane Smith earned a salary of $40,000, and she realized a capital loss from the sale of stock, in the amount of $12,000. She had no capital gains in that year. She may deduct $3000 of her capital loss against her ordinary income, reducing taxable income to $37,000 (before considering other items of income and deduction). The remaining $9000 of capital loss is carried forward until it is either absorbed by future ordinary income, offset against future capital gains, or Jane dies.

Not Subject to the Limitation

Most investment in real estate escapes the harsh treatment of capital losses because there is a rule which says that "property used in a trade or business" is generally not subject to the limitation on capital losses. Losses on the *sale* of property used in a trade or business can be deducted against any type of income in an unlimited amount.

Generally speaking, improved real estate which is held for production of rental income is considered property used in a trade or business for this purpose. Vacant land held solely for speculative appreciation in value, however, is normally classified as a capital asset that is not used in a trade or business. In the pre-1986 days, rental real estate got the best of both worlds, capital gains in "gain" years and ordinary losses in "loss years." (However, if losses were realized before gains, gains on real estate sales in the next several years would be recharacterized as ordinary income, up to the amount of ordinary loss previously deducted.)

Residences

The most common type of real estate owned by individuals—property that they occupy as a residence, whether primary or secondary—does not, however, get the benefit of any deduction. Losses on the sale of a residence are treated as nondeductible personal expenses, analogous to food, clothing, or entertainment, even though gains on such sales are included as capital gains unless they qualify for the $125,000 once-in-a-lifetime exclusion or the "rollover rule" described in Chapter 4.

Mixed-Use Buildings

If a building is used for both residential and business purposes—such as a duplex building of which one unit is occupied by the owner and the other by a tenant—the loss will be apportioned between the two units on a reasonable basis, and the loss on the rental unit can be deducted.

Example.   Harry Jones owned a duplex, which he purchased for $200,000 in 1989. He occupied one unit and rented out the other to a tenant to whom he is not related. The two units are essentially identical. Harry deducted depreciation of $10,000 in 1989, 1990, 1991, and 1992. He sells the building at the beginning of 1993 for $150,000. Harry may appropriately pro rate his cost between the two units, at $100,000 for each unit. The rental unit's basis is adjusted downward to $90,000 because of depreciation. On sale of the building, he has a nondeductible loss of $25,000 on the personal residence unit and a deductible loss of $15,000 on the rental unit.

Conversion

In the above example, if Harry had moved out of the residential unit before selling the building, rented out his former residential unit, and treated the move as a conversion, he might be able to deduct the loss on both units. However, he would have to determine the fair market value of the unit at the time he converted it to rental purposes. His deductible loss cannot exceed the value at the time of conversion, less depreciation after conversion, over the amount realized on sale.

Example. In the above example, assume that Harry had the building appraised at $190,000 when he moved out of the first unit and deducted $3000 in depreciation on that unit after he moved out. [His deductible loss on the former residential unit is $17,000 ($95,000, that is 50 percent of $190,000, less $3000 depreciation and $75,000 proceeds of sale).]

Future Changes

The 1993 tax law to carry out President Clinton's economic reform package returned the former capital gains benefit for high-income taxpayers because the higher rates and surcharge do not apply to capital gains.

Foreign Owners

One other important issue to note is that if a foreign person is the seller of real estate, the buyer, or his or her escrow company, is generally required to withhold, and pay over to the IRS, 10 percent of the sales price. In California, if the seller is not a California resident, there is a requirement that $3^1/3$ percent of the selling price be withheld and paid to the Franchise Tax Board. Some other states have similar requirements.

Sellers may request exemptions from withholding, or elimination of withholding, but only if they show that their gain on the sale of the property, multiplied by the applicable tax rate, is less than the amount of the required withholding.

Tip

A buyer need not arrange for federal withholding if the purchase price of the property is less than $300,000 and he or she intends to use it as a residence. Likewise, no withholding is required if the transferor provides a "nonforeign affidavit," unless the buyer has actual knowledge that the affidavit is false or receives a notice from an agent of the seller that the affidavit is false.

Imputed Interest

Another point to note is that if the seller of real estate takes back a promissory note for all or part of the consideration for the sale, and the promissory note does not bear adequate interest as defined by the tax law and the IRS, some of the payments on the note will be recharacterized as interest, which would not qualify for favorable capital gains rates, even the modest 3 percent favoritism now in the law. However, in today's market, interest rates are so low that this is only rarely a problem.

Tax Credits

In addition to deductions, some owners of real estate benefit from tax credits that are allowed for certain types of costs and expenses. A credit differs from a deduction because it directly offsets the tax liability, rather than simply reducing the amount of taxable income, a fraction of which constitutes the tax liability (based on the applicable tax rate schedule or tax table). There are two major credits:

1. For investment in low-income housing
2. For qualified rehabilitation expenses applicable to older buildings

Low-Income Housing Credit

The low-income credit is taken over a 10-year period, at a rate that ranges between 8 and 9 percent per year. The IRS sets new rates on a monthly basis, which take into account prevailing interest rates and are intended to provide the owner with a credit that has a *present value* equal to 70 percent of the cost of the project.

The tax law includes numerous very specific rules that are designed to ensure that units constructed with the aid of the credit will be available for and actually used by families who have low incomes. Also, the credit cannot be claimed automatically. Each state has a "volume cap" based primarily on population. Credits are only allowable up to the amount of the volume cap for the year. Credits are allocated by state housing or similar agencies. Unused credits for any year are placed into a "national pool" and are allocated by the Department of Housing and Urban Development.

Rehabilitation Credit

The rehabilitation credit was available for a portion of the cost of reconstructing or rehabilitating qualifying structures of considerable age. The credit is at the rate of either 10 or 20 percent of qualifying costs incurred in effecting rehabilitations, the percentage varying with the particular type of structure. The higher credit rate is available for rehabilitation expenses affecting "certified historic structures." These are either buildings that have been designated as having historic interest or buildings located in a registered historic district, certified either by a state agency that the Interior Department has certified as having appropriate criteria for designation or by the agency that publishes the National Register.

For buildings other than certified historic structures, at least 50 percent of the external walls of the building must be retained in place as external walls, at least 75 percent of the internal walls must be retained as either internal *or* external walls, and 75 percent of internal structural framework must be retained in place. For certified historic structures, the external wall test does not apply, but rigorous design criteria designed to ensure that the building continues to exhibit the historically important characteristics must be satisfied instead.

To qualify as substantially rehabilitated, expenses constituting rehabilitations, during a 24-month period selected by the taxpayer, must exceed the greater of $5000 or (more importantly) the building's adjusted basis at the beginning of the period.

A major advantage of both the rehabilitation credit and the low-income credit is that there is no active participation requirement to satisfy in order to claim up to approximately $9000 of credits (equivalent to $25,000 in deductions, assuming a 36 percent tax rate).

In the case of the low-income credit, moreover, there is no phaseout rule based on net income exceeding $100,000. In the case of the rehabilitation credit, the phaseout does not begin until the taxpayer's adjusted gross income reaches $200,000, while the allowance for other types of rental income begins to phase out at the $100,000 income level.

Appendix **B**

Major Changes Made by the 1993 Tax Law

In August of 1993, Congress passed and President Clinton signed a budget bill which included a number of tax law changes that significantly affect real estate. While many of these changes are incorporated into the text of this book where appropriate, they are summarized here for the benefit of those who would like to see them at a glance.

1. Under the passive/active rules, real estate losses normally cannot be used to offset income in other areas, such as from personal services. (The $25,000 exclusion applies here as noted in Chapter 8.) An exception was created in the 1993 law. Effective as of 1994, *real estate professionals* may offset losses from real estate activities in which they materially participate if more than half of the total personal services are performed in real property businesses in which the individual spends more than 750 hours of actual work. A real property business means any real property development, redevelopment, construction, reconstruction, acquisition, conversion, rental oper-

ation, management, leasing, or brokerage trade or business. These fortunate individuals will be able to offset their real estate losses against all of their income, not just that derived from real property business.

2. Depreciable life for commercial property placed in service on or after May 13, 1993, has been increased to 39 years, unless the property is placed in service before January 1, 1994, pursuant to a contract that was binding on the taxpayer on May 13, 1993, or construction of new property had actually commenced before May 19, 1993.

3. Investors who find it necessary to restructure debt that they incurred in order to acquire real property will benefit from a new rule that allows them to treat any reduction of debt as a lowering of basis rather than as triggering immediate income as is true, in most cases, under prior law. This new rule is effective retroactive to the beginning of 1993.

4. The low-income housing credit has been permanently extended, retroactive to June 30, 1992, and its provisions have been liberalized in certain respects.

5. Pension funds and other tax-exempt entities have been aided by rules that reduce or eliminate the chance that income from real estate will be treated as taxable unrelated business income. This is especially true for acquisitions of property from financial institutions in conservatorship or receivership, the RTC, and similar entities.

Appendix **C**

Tax Forms

For those who are involved in real estate as *investors,* the *preparation* of actual tax forms used to file federal income taxes is probably best left to professionals. This is not to say that you, as an individual and owner of a single rental property, can't fill out your own Schedule E and other related forms and properly refer them to your 1040. It's just that with the different depreciation schedules, the varying tax filing requirements of your particular property and with the convoluted language the Internal Revenue Service uses (in its attempt to simplify the filling out of its forms), the few dollars a tax preparer charges can often be offset by the tax savings he or she may find for you. This is much more so the case if you have multiple properties, sales, trades, and so on.

Nevertheless, it can be helpful to have the actual forms at hand when planning investment and tax strategies. Knowing which forms are often used and seeing the sorts of items the government asks for can help in making decisions today which will be reflected in tax consequences tomorrow.

Therefore, following are tax forms relating to real estate which may typically be filed with your federal income taxes. *Note:* Not all forms will need to be filed by everyone. Indeed, only one or two or perhaps none may be necessary. But, if they apply to you, just knowing what these forms look like and what's on them can be very helpful indeed.

SCHEDULE D
(Form 1040)

Department of the Treasury
Internal Revenue Service (X)

Name(s) shown on Form 1040

Capital Gains and Losses

(And Reconciliation of Forms 1099-B for Bartering Transactions)

▶ Attach to Form 1040.   ▶ See Instructions for Schedule D (Form 1040).

▶ For more space to list transactions for lines 1a and 9a, get Schedule D-1 (Form 1040).

OMB No. 1545-0074

19**92**

Attachment
Sequence No. **12A**

Your social security number

Caution: *Add the following amounts reported to you for 1992 on Forms 1099-B and 1099-S (or on substitute statements):* **(a)** *proceeds from transactions involving stocks, bonds, and other securities, and* **(b)** *gross proceeds from real estate transactions not reported on another form or schedule. If this total does not equal the total of lines 1c and 9c, column (d), attach a statement explaining the difference.*

Part I   Short-Term Capital Gains and Losses—Assets Held One Year or Less

(a) Description of property (Example, 100 shares 7% preferred of "XYZ" Co.)	(b) Date acquired (Mo., day, yr.)	(c) Date sold (Mo., day, yr.)	(d) Sales price (see page D-2)	(e) Cost or other basis (see page D-3)	(f) LOSS If (e) is more than (d), subtract (d) from (e)	(g) GAIN If (d) is more than (e), subtract (e) from (d)
1a Stocks, Bonds, Other Securities, and Real Estate. Include Form 1099-B and 1099-S Transactions. See page D-3.						
1b Amounts from Schedule D-1, line 1b. Attach Schedule D-1						

1c Total of All Sales Price Amounts.
Add column (d) of lines 1a and 1b . . ▶ **1c**

1d Other Transactions.

2 Short-term gain from sale or exchange of your home from Form 2119, line 17 or 23 .	**2**		
3 Short-term gain from installment sales from Form 6252, line 26 or 37	**3**		
4 Short-term gain or (loss) from like-kind exchanges from Form 8824	**4**		
5 Net short-term gain or (loss) from partnerships, S corporations, and fiduciaries .	**5**		
6 Short-term capital loss carryover from 1991 Schedule D, line 36	**6**		
7 Add lines 1a, 1b, 1d, and 2 through 6, in columns (f) and (g).	**7** (	)	
8 **Net short-term capital gain or (loss).** Combine columns (f) and (g) of line 7		**8**	

Part II   Long-Term Capital Gains and Losses—Assets Held More Than One Year

(a)	(b)	(c)	(d)	(e)	(f)	(g)
9a Stocks, Bonds, Other Securities, and Real Estate. Include Form 1099-B and 1099-S Transactions. See page D-3.						
9b Amounts from Schedule D-1, line 9b. Attach Schedule D-1						

9c Total of All Sales Price Amounts.
Add column (d) of lines 9a and 9b . . ▶ **9c**

9d Other Transactions.

10 Long-term gain from sale or exchange of your home from Form 2119, line 17 or 23 .	**10**		
11 Long-term gain from installment sales from Form 6252, line 26 or 37	**11**		
12 Long-term gain or (loss) from like-kind exchanges from Form 8824.	**12**		
13 Net long-term gain or (loss) from partnerships, S corporations, and fiduciaries .	**13**		
14 Capital gain distributions	**14**		
15 Gain from Form 4797, line 8 or 10	**15**		
16 Long-term capital loss carryover from 1991 Schedule D, line 43	**16**		
17 Add lines 9a, 9b, 9d, and 10 through 16, in columns (f) and (g).	**17** (	)	
18 **Net long-term capital gain or (loss).** Combine columns (f) and (g) of line 17		**18**	

For Paperwork Reduction Act Notice, see Form 1040 Instructions.   Cat. No. 11338H   Schedule D (Form 1040) 1992

123

Figure C-1. Schedule D.

Schedule D (Form 1040) 1992   Attachment Sequence No. **12A**   Page **2**

Name(s) shown on Form 1040. Do not enter name and social security number if shown on other side.   Your social security number

Part III   Summary of Parts I and II

19 Combine lines 8 and 18 and enter the net gain or (loss). If a gain, also enter the gain on Form 1040, line 13 . . . . | **19**

Note: If both lines 18 and 19 are gains, see Part IV below.

20 If line 19 is a (loss), enter here and as a (loss) on Form 1040, line 13, the **smaller** of:
a The (loss) on line 19; **or**
b ($3,000) or, if married filing a separate return, ($1,500) . . . . | **20** |(   )

Note: When figuring whether line 20a or 20b is **smaller**, treat both numbers as positive.
Complete Part V if the loss on line 19 is more than the loss on line 20 OR if Form 1040, line 37, is zero.

Part IV   Tax Computation Using Maximum Capital Gains Rate

USE THIS PART TO FIGURE YOUR TAX ONLY IF BOTH LINES 18 AND 19 ARE GAINS, AND:

You checked filing status box:	AND	Form 1040, line 37, is over:	You checked filing status box:	AND	Form 1040, line 37, is over:
1		$51,900	3		$43,250
2 or 5		$86,500	4		$74,150

21 Enter the amount from Form 1040, line 37 . . . . | **21**
22 Enter the **smaller** of line 18 or line 19 . . . . | **22**
23 Subtract line 22 from line 21 . . . . | **23**
24 Enter: $21,450 if you checked filing status box 1; $35,800 if you checked filing status box 2 or 5; $17,900 if you checked filing status box 3; or $28,750 if you checked filing status box 4 . . . . | **24**
25 Enter the **greater** of line 23 or line 24 . . . . | **25**
26 Subtract line 25 from line 21 . . . . | **26**
27 Figure the tax on the amount on line 25. Use the Tax Table or Tax Rate Schedules, whichever applies | **27**
28 Multiply line 26 by 28% (.28) . . . . | **28**
29 Add lines 27 and 28. Enter here and on Form 1040, line 38, and check the box for Schedule D . | **29**

Part V   Capital Loss Carryovers from 1992 to 1993

30 Enter the amount from Form 1040, line 35. If a loss, enclose the amount in parentheses . . . . | **30**
31 Enter the loss from line 20 as a positive amount . . . . | **31**
32 Combine lines 30 and 31. If zero or less, enter -0- . . . . | **32**
33 Enter the **smaller** of line 31 or line 32 . . . . | **33**

Note: If both lines 8 and 20 are losses, go to line 34; otherwise, skip lines 34-38.

34 Enter the loss from line 8 as a positive amount . . . . | **34**
35 Enter the gain, if any, from line 18 . . . . | **35**
36 Enter the amount from line 33 . . . . | **36**
37 Add lines 35 and 36 . . . . | **37**
38 Short-term capital loss carryover to **1993**. Subtract line 37 from line 34. If zero or less, enter -0- . | **38**

Note: If both lines 18 and 20 are losses, go to line 39; otherwise, skip lines 39-45.

39 Enter the loss from line 18 as a positive amount . . . . | **39**
40 Enter the gain, if any, from line 8 . . . . | **40**
41 Enter the amount from line 33 . . . . . | **41**
42 Enter the amount, if any, from line 34 . . | **42**
43 Subtract line 42 from line 41. If zero or less, enter -0- . . . . | **43**
44 Add lines 40 and 43 . . . . | **44**
45 Long-term capital loss carryover to **1993**. Subtract line 44 from line 39. If zero or less, enter -0- . | **45**

Part VI   Election Not To Use the Installment Method. Complete this part **only** if you elect out of the installment method and report a note or other obligation at less than full face value.

46 Check here if you elect out of the installment method . . . . ▶ ☐
47 Enter the face amount of the note or other obligation . . . . ▶ ....
48 Enter the percentage of valuation of the note or other obligation . . . . ▶ .... %

Part VII   Reconciliation of Forms 1099-B for Bartering Transactions. Complete this part **only** if you received one or more Forms 1099-B or substitute statements reporting **bartering income.** | Amount of bartering income from Form 1099-B or substitute statement reported on form or schedule

49 Form 1040, line 22 . . . . | **49**
50 Schedule C, C-EZ, D, E, or F (specify) ▶ .... | **50**
51 Other form or schedule (identify). If nontaxable, indicate reason—attach additional sheets if necessary: .... | **51**
52 **Total.** Add lines 49 through 51. This amount should be the same as the total bartering income on all Forms 1099-B and substitute statements received for bartering transactions . . . . | **52**

SCHEDULE D-1
(Form 1040)

Department of the Treasury
Internal Revenue Service

Continuation Sheet for Schedule D
(Form 1040)
▶ See Instructions for Schedule D (Form 1040).
▶ Attach to Schedule D if you need more space to list transactions for lines 1a and 9a.

OMB No. 1545-0074

19**92**

Attachment
Sequence No. **12B**

Name(s) shown on Form 1040

Your social security number

Part I   Short-Term Capital Gains and Losses—Assets Held One Year or Less

(a) Description of property (Example, 100 shares 7% preferred of "XYZ" Co.)	(b) Date acquired (Mo., day, yr.)	(c) Date sold (Mo., day, yr.)	(d) Sales price (see page D-2)	(e) Cost or other basis (see page D-3)	(f) LOSS If (e) is more than (d), subtract (d) from (e)	(g) GAIN If (d) is more than (e), subtract (e) from (d)
1a Stocks, Bonds, Other Securities, and Real Estate. Include Form 1099-B and 1099-S Transactions. See page D-3.						

1b Totals. Add columns (d), (f), and (g). Enter here and on Schedule D (Form 1040), line 1b ▶ **1b**

For Paperwork Reduction Act Notice, see Form 1040 Instructions.

Cat. No. 10424K

Schedule D-1 (Form 1040) 1992

125

Figure C-2. Schedule D-1.

Schedule D-1 (Form 1040) 1992 Attachment Sequence No. **12B** Page **2**

Name(s) shown on Form 1040. Do not enter name and social security number if shown on other side.

Your social security number

Part II Long-Term Capital Gains and Losses—Assets Held More Than One Year

(a) Description of property (Example, 100 shares 7% preferred of "XYZ" Co.)	(b) Date acquired (Mo., day, yr.)	(c) Date sold (Mo., day, yr.)	(d) Sales price (see page D-2)	(e) Cost or other basis (see page D-3)	(f) LOSS If (e) is more than (d), subtract (d) from (e)	(g) GAIN If (d) is more than (e), subtract (e) from (d)
9a Stocks, Bonds, Other Securities, and Real Estate. Include Form 1099-B and 1099-S Transactions. See page D-3.						

9b Totals. Add columns (d), (f), and (g). Enter here and on Schedule D (Form 1040), line 9b . ▶ **9b**

126

SCHEDULE E
(Form 1040)

Department of the Treasury
Internal Revenue Service   (X)

Supplemental Income and Loss

(From rental real estate, royalties, partnerships, estates, trusts, REMICs, etc.)
► Attach to Form 1040 or Form 1041.
► See Instructions for Schedule E (Form 1040).

OMB No. 1545-0074

19**92**

Attachment
Sequence No. **13**

Name(s) shown on return

Your social security number

Part I   **Income or Loss From Rental Real Estate and Royalties**   Note: *Report income and expenses from the rental of personal property on Schedule C or C-EZ. Report farm rental income or loss from Form 4835 on page 2, line 39.*

1	Show the kind and location of each **rental real estate property:**			2 For each rental real estate property listed on line 1, did you or your family use it for personal purposes for more than the greater of 14 days or 10% of the total days rented at fair rental value during the tax year? (See page E-1.)		Yes	No
A	....			A			
B	....			B			
C	....			C			

Income:		Properties			Totals
		A	**B**	**C**	(Add columns A, B, and C.)
3 Rents received	3				3	
4 Royalties received	4				4	
Expenses:					
5 Advertising	5				
6 Auto and travel (see page E-2) .	6				
7 Cleaning and maintenance . . .	7				
8 Commissions	8				
9 Insurance	9				
10 Legal and other professional fees	10				
11 Management fees	11				
12 Mortgage interest paid to banks, etc. (see page E-2)	12				12	
13 Other interest	13				
14 Repairs	14				
15 Supplies	15				
16 Taxes	16				
17 Utilities	17				
18 Other (list) ►	18				
19 Add lines 5 through 18	19				19	
20 Depreciation expense or depletion (see page E-2)	20				20	
21 Total expenses. Add lines 19 and 20	21				
22 Income or (loss) from rental real estate or royalty properties. Subtract line 21 from line 3 (rents) or line 4 (royalties). If the result is a (loss), see page E-2 to find out if you must file **Form 6198**. . .	22				
23 Deductible rental real estate loss. **Caution:** *Your rental real estate loss on line 22 may be limited. See page E-3 to find out if you must file Form 8582*	23	( )	( )	( )	

24	**Income.** Add positive amounts shown on line 22. **Do not** include any losses	24	
25	**Losses.** Add royalty losses from line 22 and rental real estate losses from line 23. Enter the total losses here	25	( )
26	**Total** rental real estate and royalty income or (loss). Combine lines 24 and 25. Enter the result here. If Parts II, III, IV, and line 39 on page 2 do not apply to you, also enter this amount on Form 1040, line 18. Otherwise, include this amount in the total on line 40 on page 2	26	

For Paperwork Reduction Act Notice, see Form 1040 instructions.   Cat. No. 11344L   Schedule E (Form 1040) 1992

127

Figure C-3. Schedule E.

Schedule E (Form 1040) 1992 — Attachment Sequence No. **13** — Page **2**

Name(s) shown on return. Do not enter name and social security number if shown on other side. | Your social security number

Note: *If you report amounts from farming or fishing on Schedule E, you must enter your gross income from those activities on line 41 below.*

Part II   Income or Loss From Partnerships and S Corporations

If you report a loss from an at-risk activity, you MUST check either column **(e)** or **(f)** of line 27 to describe your investment in the activity. See page E-3. If you check column **(f)**, you must attach **Form 6198**.

27	(a) Name	(b) Enter P for partnership; S for S corporation	(c) Check if foreign partnership	(d) Employer identification number	Investment At Risk?	
					(e) All is at risk	(f) Some is not at risk
A						
B						
C						
D						
E						

	Passive Income and Loss		Nonpassive Income and Loss		
	(g) Passive loss allowed (attach Form 8582 if required)	(h) Passive income from Schedule K-1	(i) Nonpassive loss from Schedule K-1	(j) Section 179 expense deduction from Form 4562	(k) Nonpassive income from Schedule K-1
A					
B					
C					
D					
E					
28a Totals					
b Totals					

29	Add columns (h) and (k) of line 28a	29	
30	Add columns (g), (i), and (j) of line 28b	30	( )
31	Total partnership and S corporation income or (loss). Combine lines 29 and 30. Enter the result here and include in the total on line 40 below	31	

Part III   Income or Loss From Estates and Trusts

32	(a) Name	(b) Employer identification number
A		
B		
C		

	Passive Income and Loss		Nonpassive Income and Loss	
	(c) Passive deduction or loss allowed (attach Form 8582 if required)	(d) Passive income from Schedule K-1	(e) Deduction or loss from Schedule K-1	(f) Other income from Schedule K-1
A				
B				
C				
33a Totals				
b Totals				

34	Add columns (d) and (f) of line 33a	34	
35	Add columns (c) and (e) of line 33b	35	( )
36	Total estate and trust income or (loss). Combine lines 34 and 35. Enter the result here and include in the total on line 40 below	36	

Part IV   Income or Loss From Real Estate Mortgage Investment Conduits (REMICs)—Residual Holder

37	(a) Name	(b) Employer identification number	(c) Excess inclusion from Schedules Q, line 2c (see page E-4)	(d) Taxable income (net loss) from Schedules Q, line 1b	(e) Income from Schedules Q, line 3b

38	Combine columns (d) and (e) only. Enter the result here and include in the total on line 40 below	38	

Part V   Summary

39	Net farm rental income or (loss) from Form 4835. Also, complete line 41 below	39	
40	TOTAL income or (loss). Combine lines 26, 31, 36, 38, and 39. Enter the result here and on Form 1040, line 18 . . . . ▶	40	
41	Reconciliation of Farming and Fishing Income: Enter your **gross** farming and fishing income reported in Parts II and III and on line 39 (see page E-4) 41		

Form **4562**	**Depreciation and Amortization**	OMB No. 1545-0172
Department of the Treasury Internal Revenue Service (X)	**(Including Information on Listed Property)** ▶ See separate instructions. ▶ Attach this form to your return.	19**92** Attachment Sequence No. **67**
Name(s) shown on return		Identifying number

Business or activity to which this form relates

Part I   **Election To Expense Certain Tangible Property (Section 179)** (Note: *If you have any "Listed Property," complete Part V before you complete Part I.)*

1	Maximum dollar limitation (see instructions)	**1**	$10,000
2	Total cost of section 179 property placed in service during the tax year (see instructions) . .	**2**	
3	Threshold cost of section 179 property before reduction in limitation	**3**	$200,000
4	Reduction in limitation. Subtract line 3 from line 2, but do not enter less than -0-	**4**	
5	Dollar limitation for tax year. Subtract line 4 from line 1, but do not enter less than -0- . .	**5**	

(a) Description of property	(b) Cost	(c) Elected cost	
6			

7	Listed property. Enter amount from line 26.	**7**	
8	Total elected cost of section 179 property. Add amounts in column (c), lines 6 and 7 . . .	**8**	
9	Tentative deduction. Enter the smaller of line 5 or line 8	**9**	
10	Carryover of disallowed deduction from 1991 (see instructions)	**10**	
11	Taxable income limitation. Enter the smaller of taxable income or line 5 (see instructions) . .	**11**	
12	Section 179 expense deduction. Add lines 9 and 10, but do not enter more than line 11 . .	**12**	
13	Carryover of disallowed deduction to 1993. Add lines 9 and 10, less line 12 ▶	**13**	

Note: *Do not use Part II or Part III below for automobiles, certain other vehicles, cellular telephones, computers, or property used for entertainment, recreation, or amusement (listed property). Instead, use Part V for listed property.*

Part II   **MACRS Depreciation For Assets Placed in Service ONLY During Your 1992 Tax Year (Do Not Include Listed Property)**

(a) Classification of property	(b) Month and year placed in service	(c) Basis for depreciation (business/investment use only—see instructions)	(d) Recovery period	(e) Convention	(f) Method	(g) Depreciation deduction
14 General Depreciation System (GDS) (see instructions):						
a 3-year property						
b 5-year property						
c 7-year property						
d 10-year property						
e 15-year property						
f 20-year property						
g Residential rental property			27.5 yrs.	MM	S/L	
			27.5 yrs.	MM	S/L	
h Nonresidential real property			31.5 yrs.	MM	S/L	
			31.5 yrs.	MM	S/L	
15 Alternative Depreciation System (ADS) (see instructions):						
a Class life					S/L	
b 12-year			12 yrs.		S/L	
c 40-year			40 yrs.	MM	S/L	

Part III   **Other Depreciation (Do Not Include Listed Property)**

16	GDS and ADS deductions for assets placed in service in tax years beginning before 1992 (see instructions)	**16**	
17	Property subject to section 168(f)(1) election (see instructions)	**17**	
18	ACRS and other depreciation (see instructions)	**18**	

Part IV   **Summary**

19	Listed property. Enter amount from line 25.	**1**	
20	**Total.** Add deductions on line 12, lines 14 and 15 in column (g), and lines 16 through 19. Enter here and on the appropriate lines of your return. (Partnerships and S corporations—see instructions)	**20**	
21	For assets shown above and placed in service during the current year, enter the portion of the basis attributable to section 263A costs (see instructions)	**21**	

For Paperwork Reduction Act Notice, see page 1 of the separate instructions.   Cat. No. 12906N   Form **4562** (1992)

Figure C-4. Form 4562.

Form 4562 (1992)   Page **2**

Part V **Listed Property—Automobiles, Certain Other Vehicles, Cellular Telephones, Computers, and Property Used for Entertainment, Recreation, or Amusement**

For any vehicle for which you are using the standard mileage rate or deducting lease expense, complete only 22a, 22b, columns (a) through (c) of Section A, all of Section B, and Section C if applicable.

Section A—Depreciation (Caution: *See instructions for limitations for automobiles.)*

22a Do you have evidence to support the business/investment use claimed? ☐ Yes ☐ No │ 22b If "Yes," is the evidence written? ☐ Yes ☐ No

(a) Type of property (list vehicles first)	(b) Date placed in service	(c) Business/ investment use percentage	(d) Cost or other basis	(e) Basis for depreciation (business/investment use only)	(f) Recovery period	(g) Method/ Convention	(h) Depreciation deduction	(i) Elected section 179 cost
23 Property used more than 50% in a qualified business use (see instructions):								
		%						
		%						
		%						
24 Property used 50% or less in a qualified business use (see instructions):								
		%			S/L –			
		%			S/L –	—		
		%			S/L –			

25 Add amounts in column (h). Enter the total here and on line 19, page 1 . . . . . . **25**
26 Add amounts in column (i). Enter the total here and on line 7, page 1 . . . . **26**

Section B—Information Regarding Use of Vehicles—*If you deduct expenses for vehicles:*

• *Always complete this section for vehicles used by a sole proprietor, partner, or other "more than 5% owner," or related person.*
• *If you provided vehicles to your employees, first answer the questions in Section C to see if you meet an exception to completing this section for those vehicles.*

	(a) Vehicle 1		(b) Vehicle 2		(c) Vehicle 3		(d) Vehicle 4		(e) Vehicle 5		(f) Vehicle 6	
27 Total business/investment miles driven during the year (DO NOT include commuting miles)												
28 Total commuting miles driven during the year												
29 Total other personal (noncommuting) miles driven												
30 Total miles driven during the year. Add lines 27 through 29.												
	Yes	No	Yes	No	Yes	No	Yes	No	Yes	No	Yes	No
31 Was the vehicle available for personal use during off-duty hours?												
32 Was the vehicle used primarily by a more than 5% owner or related person?												
33 Is another vehicle available for personal use?												

Section C—Questions for Employers Who Provide Vehicles for Use by Their Employees
Answer these questions to determine if you meet an exception to completing Section B. **Note:** *Section B must always be completed for vehicles used by sole proprietors, partners, or other more than 5% owners or related persons.*

	Yes	No
34 Do you maintain a written policy statement that prohibits all personal use of vehicles, including commuting, by your employees?		
35 Do you maintain a written policy statement that prohibits personal use of vehicles, except commuting, by your employees? (See instructions for vehicles used by corporate officers, directors, or 1% or more owners.)		
36 Do you treat all use of vehicles by employees as personal use?		
37 Do you provide more than five vehicles to your employees and retain the information received from your employees concerning the use of the vehicles?		
38 Do you meet the requirements concerning qualified automobile demonstration use (see instructions)? . . .		
Note: *If your answer to 34, 35, 36, 37, or 38 is "Yes," you need not complete Section B for the covered vehicles.*		

Part VI **Amortization**

(a) Description of costs	(b) Date amortization begins	(c) Amortizable amount	(d) Code section	(e) Amortization period or percentage	(f) Amortization for this year
39 Amortization of costs that begins during your 1992 tax year:					

40 Amortization of costs that began before 1992 . . . . **40**
41 Total. Enter here and on "Other Deductions" or "Other Expenses" line of your return . . . **41**

Table A—General Depreciation System
Method: 200% declining balance switching to straight line
Convention: Half-year

Year	If the recovery period is:			
	3 yrs.	5 yrs.	7 yrs.	10 yrs.
1	33.33%	20.00%	14.29%	10.00%
2	44.45%	32.00%	24.49%	18.00%
3	14.81%	19.20%	17.49%	14.40%
4	7.41%	11.52%	12.49%	11.52%
5		11.52%	8.93%	9.22%
6		5.76%	8.92%	7.37%
7			8.93%	6.55%

Table B—General and Alternative Depreciation System
Method: 150% declining balance switching to straight line
Convention: Half-year

Year	If the recovery period is:					
	5 yrs.	7 yrs.	10 yrs.	12 yrs.	15 yrs.	20 yrs.
1	15.00%	10.71%	7.50%	6.25%	5.00%	3.750%
2	25.50%	19.13%	13.88%	11.72%	9.50%	7.219%
3	17.85%	15.03%	11.79%	10.25%	8.55%	6.677%
4	16.66%	12.25%	10.02%	8.97%	7.70%	6.177%
5	16.66%	12.25%	8.74%	7.85%	6.93%	5.713%
6	8.33%	12.25%	8.74%	7.33%	6.23%	5.285%
7		12.25%	8.74%	7.33%	5.90%	4.888%

Table C—General Depreciation System
Method: Straight line
Convention: Mid-month
Recovery period: 27.5 years

Year	The month in the 1st recovery year the property is placed in service:											
	1	2	3	4	5	6	7	8	9	10	11	12
1	3.485%	3.182%	2.879%	2.576%	2.273%	1.970%	1.667%	1.364%	1.061%	0.758%	0.455%	0.152%
2–8	3.636%	3.636%	3.636%	3.636%	3.636%	3.636%	3.636%	3.636%	3.636%	3.636%	3.636%	3.636%

Table D—General Depreciation System
Method: Straight line
Convention: Mid-month
Recovery period: 31.5 years

Year	The month in the 1st recovery year the property is placed in service:											
	1	2	3	4	5	6	7	8	9	10	11	12
1	3.042%	2.778%	2.513%	2.249%	1.984%	1.720%	1.455%	1.190%	0.926%	0.661%	0.397%	0.132%
2–7	3.175%	3.175%	3.175%	3.175%	3.175%	3.175%	3.175%	3.175%	3.175%	3.175%	3.175%	3.175%

Table E—Limitations for automobiles

Year of Deduction	after: but before:	If placed in service:						
		6/18/84 1/1/85	12/31/84 4/3/85	4/2/85 1/1/87	12/31/86 1/1/89	12/31/88 1/1/91	12/31/90 1/1/92	12/31/91 1/1/93
1st tax year		4,000	4,100	3,200	2,560	2,660	2,660	2,760
2nd tax year		6,000	6,200	4,800	4,100	4,200	4,300	4,400
3rd tax year		6,000	6,200	4,800	2,450	2,550	2,550	2,650
each succeeding tax year		6,000	6,200	4,800	1,475	1,475	1,575	1,575

Figure C-5. Depreciation tables and worksheet.

Depreciation Worksheet

Description of Property	Date Placed in Service	Cost or Other Basis	Business/ Investment Use %	Section 179 Deduction	Depreciation Prior Years	Basis for Depreciation	Method/ Convention	Recovery Period	Rate or Table %	Depreciation Deduction

286

194

Appendix C

Form **4797**	**Sales of Business Property** (Also Involuntary Conversions and Recapture Amounts Under Sections 179 and 280F) ▶ Attach to your tax return. ▶ See separate instructions.	OMB No. 1545-0184
Department of the Treasury Internal Revenue Service (X)		**1992** Attachment Sequence No. 27

Name(s) shown on return | Identifying number

1   Enter here the gross proceeds from the sale or exchange of real estate reported to you for 1992 on Form(s) 1099-S (or a substitute statement) that you will be including on line 2, 11, or 22 . . . . | **1**

Part I   Sales or Exchanges of Property Used in a Trade or Business and Involuntary Conversions From Other Than Casualty or Theft—Property Held More Than 1 Year

(a) Description of property	(b) Date acquired (mo., day, yr.)	(c) Date sold (mo., day, yr.)	(d) Gross sales price	(e) Depreciation allowed or allowable since acquisition	(f) Cost or other basis, plus improvements and expense of sale	(g) LOSS ((f) minus the sum of (d) and (e))	(h) GAIN ((d) plus (e) minus (f))
2							

3   Gain, if any, from Form 4684, line 39 . . . . | **3** |
4   Section 1231 gain from installment sales from Form 6252, line 26 or 37 . . . . | **4** |
5   Section 1231 gain or (loss) from like-kind exchanges from Form 8824 . . . . | **5** |
6   Gain, if any, from line 34, from other than casualty or theft . . . . | **6** |
7   Add lines 2 through 6 in columns (g) and (h) . . . . | **7** ( )
8   Combine columns (g) and (h) of line 7. Enter gain or (loss) here, and on the appropriate line as follows: . . . . | **8**

    Partnerships—Enter the gain or (loss) on Form 1065, Schedule K, line 6. Skip lines 9, 10, 12, and 13 below.

    S corporations—Report the gain or (loss) following the instructions for Form 1120S, Schedule K, lines 5 and 6. Skip lines 9, 10, 12, and 13 below, unless line 8 is a gain and the S corporation is subject to the capital gains tax.

    All others—If line 8 is zero or a loss, enter the amount on line 12 below and skip lines 9 and 10. If line 8 is a gain and you did not have any prior year section 1231 losses, or they were recaptured in an earlier year, enter the gain as a long-term capital gain on Schedule D and skip lines 9, 10, and 13 below.

9   Nonrecaptured net section 1231 losses from prior years (see instructions) . . . . | **9** |
10   Subtract line 9 from line 8. If zero or less, enter -0-. Also enter on the appropriate line as follows (see instructions): | **10** |

    S corporations—Enter this amount (if more than zero) on Schedule D (Form 1120S), line 13, and skip lines 12 and 13 below.

    All others—If line 10 is zero, enter the amount from line 8 on line 13 below. If line 10 is more than zero, enter the amount from line 9 on line 13 below, and enter the amount from line 10 as a long-term capital gain on Schedule D.

Part II   Ordinary Gains and Losses

11   Ordinary gains and losses not included on lines 12 through 18 (include property held 1 year or less):

12   Loss, if any, from line 8 . . . . | **12** |
13   Gain, if any, from line 8, or amount from line 9 if applicable . . . . | **13** |
14   Gain, if any, from line 33 . . . . | **14** |
15   Net gain or (loss) from Form 4684, lines 31 and 38a . . . . | **15** |
16   Ordinary gain from installment sales from Form 6252, line 25 or 36 . . . . | **16** |
17   Ordinary gain or (loss) from like-kind exchanges from Form 8824 . . . . | **17** |
18   Recapture of section 179 expense deduction for partners and S corporation shareholders from property dispositions by partnerships and S corporations (see instructions) . . . . . . | **18** |
19   Add lines 11 through 18 in columns (g) and (h) . . . . | **19** ( )
20   Combine columns (g) and (h) of line 19. Enter gain or (loss) here, and on the appropriate line as follows: . . | **20**
  a   For all except individual returns: Enter the gain or (loss) from line 20 on the return being filed.
  b   For individual returns:
    (1)   If the loss on line 12 includes a loss from Form 4684, line 35, column (b)(ii), enter that part of the loss here and on line 20 of Schedule A (Form 1040). Identify as from "Form 4797, line 20b(1)." See instructions . . . . | **20b(1)**
    (2)   Redetermine the gain or (loss) on line 20, excluding the loss, if any, on line 20b(1). Enter here and on Form 1040, line 15 . | **20b(2)**

For Paperwork Reduction Act Notice, see page 1 of separate Instructions.   Cat. No. 13086I   Form **4797** (1992)

289

Figure C-6. Form 4797.

Form 4797 (1992)   Page **2**

Part III   Gain From Disposition of Property Under Sections 1245, 1250, 1252, 1254, and 1255

21	(a) Description of section 1245, 1250, 1252, 1254, or 1255 property:		(b) Date acquired (mo., day, yr.)	(c) Date sold (mo., day, yr.)
A				
B				
C				
D				

	Relate lines 21A through 21D to these columns ▶		Property A	Property B	Property C	Property D
22	Gross sales price (**Note:** *See line 1 before completing.*)	22				
23	Cost or other basis plus expense of sale	23				
24	Depreciation (or depletion) allowed or allowable . . .	24				
25	Adjusted basis. Subtract line 24 from line 23	25				
26	Total gain. Subtract line 25 from line 22	26				
27	**If section 1245 property:**					
a	Depreciation allowed or allowable from line 24	27a				
b	Enter the **smaller** of line 26 or 27a	27b				
28	**If section 1250 property:** If straight line depreciation was used, enter -0- on line 28g, except for a corporation subject to section 291.					
a	Additional depreciation after 1975 (see instructions) . . .	28a				
b	Applicable percentage multiplied by the **smaller** of line 26 or line 28a (see instructions)	28b				
c	Subtract line 28a from line 26. If line 26 is not more than line 28a, skip lines 28d and 28e	28c				
d	Additional depreciation after 1969 and before 1976 . . .	28d				
e	Applicable percentage multiplied by the **smaller** of line 28c or 28d (see instructions)	28e				
f	Section 291 amount (corporations only)	28f				
g	Add lines 28b, 28e, and 28f	28g				
29	**If section 1252 property:** Skip this section if you did not dispose of farmland or if this form is being completed for a partnership.					
a	Soil, water, and land clearing expenses	29a				
b	Line 29a multiplied by applicable percentage (see instructions)	29b				
c	Enter the **smaller** of line 26 or 29b	29c				
30	**If section 1254 property:**					
a	Intangible drilling and development costs, expenditures for development of mines and other natural deposits, and mining exploration costs (see instructions)	30a				
b	Enter the **smaller** of line 26 or 30a	30b				
31	**If section 1255 property:**					
a	Applicable percentage of payments excluded from income under section 126 (see instructions)	31a				
b	Enter the **smaller** of line 26 or 31a	31b				

Summary of Part III Gains. Complete property columns A through D, through line 31b before going to line 32.

32	Total gains for all properties. Add columns A through D, line 26	32	
33	Add columns A through D, lines 27b, 28g, 29c, 30b, and 31b. Enter here and on line 14. See the instructions for Part IV if this is an installment sale	33	
34	Subtract line 33 from line 32. Enter the portion from casualty or theft on Form 4684, line 33. Enter the portion from other than casualty or theft on Form 4797, line 6	34	

Part IV   Election Not to Use the Installment Method. Complete this part only if you elect out of the installment method and report a note or other obligation at less than full face value.

35	Check here if you elect out of the installment method . . . . ▶	▶ ☐
36	Enter the face amount of the note or other obligation . . . . ▶	$
37	Enter the percentage of valuation of the note or other obligation . . . . ▶	%

Part V   Recapture Amounts Under Sections 179 and 280F When Business Use Drops to 50% or Less
See instructions for Part V.

			(a) Section 179	(b) Section 280F
38	Section 179 expense deduction or depreciation allowable in prior years	38		
39	Recomputed depreciation (see instructions)	39		
40	Recapture amount. Subtract line 39 from line 38. See instructions for where to report	40		

Form **6198**	**At-Risk Limitations**	OMB No. 1545-0712
Department of the Treasury Internal Revenue Service	▶ Attach to your tax return. ▶ See separate instructions.	19**92** Attachment Sequence No. 31

Name(s) shown on return | Identifying number

Description of activity

Part I   Current Year Profit (Loss) From the Activity, Including Prior Year Nondeductible Amounts. See instructions. (Enter losses in parentheses.)

1 Ordinary income (loss) from the activity. See instructions **1**
2 Gain (loss) from the sale or other disposition of assets used in the activity (or your interest in the activity) that you initially will be reporting on:
   a Schedule D **2a**
   b Form 4797 . . . . **2b**
   c Other form or schedule **2c**
3 Other income gains from the activity from Schedule K-1 of Form 1065 or Form 1120S, whichever applies, that were not included above on lines 1 through 2c **3**
4 Other deductions or losses from the activity, including investment interest expense allowed from Form 4952, that were not used in figuring amounts on lines 1 through 3 . . . . **4** (   )
5 Current year profit (loss) from the activity. Combine lines 1 through 4. See instructions before completing the rest of this form **5**

Part II   Simplified Computation of Amount At Risk (See instructions for who may use this part.)

6 Adjusted basis (as defined in section 1011) in the activity (or adjusted basis of your interest in the activity) on the first day of the tax year. Do not enter less than zero **6**
7 Increases for the tax year **7**
8 Add lines 6 and 7 . . . . **8**
9 Decreases for the tax year **9**
10 Amount at risk. Subtract line 9 from line 8 and enter the result here ▶ **10a**
   Also, enter the result on line 10b. However, if the result is less than zero, enter -0- on line 10b and see **Pub. 925** for information on the recapture rules. **Note:** You may want to use Part III to see if the method in that part gives you a larger amount at risk. Enter the larger amount (but not less than zero) on line 20 | **10b**

Part III   Detailed Computation of Amount At Risk
(If you completed Part III of Form 6198 for 1991, see instructions for Part III before completing this part for 1992.)

11 Investment in the activity (or investment in interest in the activity) at the effective date. Do not enter less than zero **11**
12 Increases at effective date **12**
13 Add lines 11 and 12 . . . . **13**
14 Decreases at effective date **14**
15 Amount at risk (check box that applies):
   a ☐ At effective date. Subtract line 14 from line 13. Do not enter less than zero. } . . **15**
   b ☐ From 1991 Form 6198, line 19. (Do not enter the amount from line 10 of the 1991 form.) }
16 Increases since (check box that applies):
   a ☐ Effective date } **16**
   b ☐ The end of your 1991 tax year }
17 Add lines 15 and 16 . . . . **17**
18 Decreases since (check box that applies):
   a ☐ Effective date } **18**
   b ☐ The end of your 1991 tax year }
19 Amount at risk. Subtract line 18 from line 17 and enter the result here ▶ **19a**
   Also, enter the result on line 19b. However, if the result is less than zero, enter -0- on line 19b and see **Pub. 925** for information on the recapture rules. Also, enter it on line 20 if you are not using the amount from Part II **19b**

Part IV   Deductible Loss

20 Amount at risk from line 10b or 19b, whichever is larger. Do not enter less than zero **20**
   Note: If line 20 is zero, enter -0- on line 21. You do not have a deductible loss this year.
21 **Deductible loss.** Enter the smaller of the loss on line 5 or the amount on line 20. See the instructions for where to report any deductible loss and any carryover . . . . **21** (   )

Note: If this loss is from a passive activity, get **Form 8582**, Passive Activity Loss Limitations, or **Form 8810**, Corporate Passive Activity Loss and Credit Limitations, to see if the loss is allowed under the passive activity rules. If part of the loss is subject to the passive activity loss rules and part of it is not, allocate the loss and take the portion attributable to the passive activity loss rules to Form 8582 or Form 8810, whichever applies.

For Paperwork Reduction Act Notice, see page 1 of the instructions for Form 6198.   Cat. No. 50012Y   Form **6198** (1992)

Figure C-7. Form 6198.

Form **6252**	**Installment Sale Income**	OMB No. 1545-0228
Department of the Treasury Internal Revenue Service	▶ See separate instructions. ▶ Attach to your tax return. Use separate form for each sale or other disposition of property on the installment method.	19**92** Attachment Sequence No. **79**
Name(s) shown on return		**Identifying number**

1 Description of property ▶ ....

2a Date acquired (month, day, and year) ▶ |____/____/____| **b** Date sold (month, day, and year) ▶ |____/____/____|

3 Was the property sold to a related party after May 14, 1980? See instructions . . . . ☐ Yes ☐ No

4 If the answer to question 3 is "Yes," was the property a marketable security? If "Yes," complete Part III. If
"No," complete Part III for the year of sale and for 2 years after the year of sale. . . . . ☐ Yes ☐ No

Part I   **Gross Profit and Contract Price.** Complete this part for the year of sale only.

5	Selling price including mortgages and other debts. Do not include interest whether stated or unstated	**5**	
6	Mortgages and other debts the buyer assumed or took the property subject to, but not new mortgages the buyer got from a bank or other source .	**6**	
7	Subtract line 6 from line 5	**7**	
8	Cost or other basis of property sold	**8**	
9	Depreciation allowed or allowable	**9**	
10	Adjusted basis. Subtract line 9 from line 8	**10**	
11	Commissions and other expenses of sale.	**11**	
12	Income recapture from Form 4797, Part III. See instructions . .	**12**	
13	Add lines 10, 11, and 12	**13**	
14	Subtract line 13 from line 5. If zero or less, do not complete the rest of this form	**14**	
15	If the property described on line 1 above was your main home, enter the total of lines 16 and 24 from Form 2119. Otherwise, enter -0-	**15**	
16	**Gross profit.** Subtract line 15 from line 14	**16**	
17	Subtract line 13 from line 6. If zero or less, enter -0-	**17**	
18	**Contract price.** Add line 7 and line 17	**18**	

Part II   **Installment Sale Income.** Complete this part for the year of sale and any year you receive a payment or
have certain debts you must treat as a payment on installment obligations.

19	Gross profit percentage. Divide line 16 by line 18. For years after the year of sale, see instructions	**19**	
20	**For year of sale only**—Enter amount from line 17 above; otherwise, enter -0-	**20**	
21	Payments received during year. See instructions. Do not include interest whether stated or unstated	**21**	
22	Add lines 20 and 21	**22**	
23	Payments received in prior years. See instructions. Do not include interest whether stated or unstated	**23**	
24	**Installment sale income.** Multiply line 22 by line 19	**24**	
25	Part of line 24 that is ordinary income under recapture rules. See instructions	**25**	
26	Subtract line 25 from line 24. Enter here and on Schedule D or Form 4797. See instructions .	**26**	

Part III   **Related Party Installment Sale Income.** Do not complete if you received the final payment this tax year.

27 Name, address, and taxpayer identifying number of related party ....

28 Did the related party, during this tax year, resell or dispose of the property ("second disposition")? . . . ☐ Yes ☐ No

29 If the answer to question 28 is "Yes," complete lines 30 through 37 below unless one of the following conditions is
met. Check only the box that applies.

   a ☐ The second disposition was more than 2 years after the first disposition (other than dispositions
of marketable securities). If this box is checked, enter the date of disposition (month, day, year) ▶ |____/____/____|

   b ☐ The first disposition was a sale or exchange of stock to the issuing corporation.

   c ☐ The second disposition was an involuntary conversion where the threat of conversion occurred after the first disposition.

   d ☐ The second disposition occurred after the death of the original seller or buyer.

   e ☐ It can be established to the satisfaction of the Internal Revenue Service that tax avoidance was not a principal purpose
for either of the dispositions. If this box is checked, attach an explanation. See instructions.

30	Selling price of property sold by related party	**30**	
31	Enter contract price from line 18 for year of first sale	**31**	
32	Enter the **smaller** of line 30 or line 31	**32**	
33	Total payments received by the end of your 1992 tax year. Add lines 22 and 23	**33**	
34	Subtract line 33 from line 32. If zero or less, enter -0-	**34**	
35	Multiply line 34 by the gross profit percentage on line 19 for year of first sale	**35**	
36	Part of line 35 that is ordinary income under recapture rules. See instructions	**36**	
37	Subtract line 36 from line 35. Enter here and on Schedule D or Form 4797. See instructions .	**37**	

For Paperwork Reduction Act Notice, see separate instructions.   315   Cat. No. 13601R   Form **6252** (1992)

Figure C-8. Form 6252.

Form **8308** (Rev. April 1991) Department of the Treasury Internal Revenue Service	**Report of a Sale or Exchange of Certain Partnership Interests** ▶ Please print or type.	OMB No. 1545-0941 Expires 4-30-94

Name of partnership | Employer Identification number

Number, street, and room or suite no. (If a P.O. box, see instructions.)

City or town, state, and ZIP code

| **Part I** | **Transferor Information** (Beneficial owner of the partnership interest immediately before the transfer of that interest) |

Name | Identifying number

Number and street (including apt. no.)

City or town, state, and ZIP code

Notice to Transferors: *The information on this form has been supplied to the Internal Revenue Service. The transferor in a section 751(a) exchange is required to treat a portion of the gain realized from the exchange as ordinary income. For more information, see **Publication 541**, Tax Information on Partnerships.*
Statement by Transferor: *The transferor in a section 751(a) exchange is required under Regulations section 1.751-1(a)(3) to attach a statement relating to the sale or exchange to his or her return. See **Instructions to Transferors** on page 2 for further details.*

| **Part II** | **Transferee Information** (Beneficial owner of the partnership interest immediately after the transfer of that interest) |

Name | Identifying number

Number and street (including apt. no.)

City or town, state, and ZIP code

| **Part III** | **Date of Sale or Exchange of Partnership Interest** ▶   /   / |

| **Sign Here Only If You Are Filing This Form by Itself and Not with Form 1065** | Under penalties of perjury, I declare that I have examined this return, including accompanying attachments, and to the best of my knowledge and belief, it is true, correct, and complete.

▶ _____
Signature of general partner | ▶ _____
Date |

Figure C-9. Form 8308.

Tax Forms   **199**

<table>
<tr><td>Form **8824**
Department of the Treasury
Internal Revenue Service</td><td>**Like-Kind Exchanges**
(and nonrecognition of gain from conflict-of-interest sales)
▶ See separate instructions. ▶ Attach to your tax return.
▶ Use a separate form for each like-kind exchange.</td><td>OMB No. 1545-1190
19**92**
Attach't
Seq. No. **49**</td></tr>
</table>

Name(s) shown on tax return   Identifying numbe

Part I   Information on the Like-Kind Exchange

Note: *If the property described on line 1 or line 2 is real property located outside the United States, indicate the country.*

1 Description of like-kind property given up ▶ ....

2 Description of like-kind property received ▶ ....

3 Date like-kind property given up was originally acquired (month, day, year) . . . . . . | **3** | / / |
4 Date you actually transferred your property to other party (month, day, year) . . . . . | **4** | / / |
5 Date the like-kind property you received was identified (month, day, year). See instructions . | **5** | / / |
6 Date you actually received the like-kind property from other party (month, day, year) . . . | **6** | / / |
7 Was the exchange made with a related party? See instructions.
   a ☐ Yes, in this tax year   b ☐ Yes, in a prior tax year   c ☐ No. If "No," go to Part II.
8 Enter the following information about the related party:

Name   Identifying number

Address (no., street, and apt. or suite no., rural route, or P.O. box no. if mail is not delivered to street address)

City or town, state, and ZIP code   Relationship to you

9 During this tax year, did the related party sell or dispose of the like-kind property received from you in the
   exchange? . . . . ☐ Yes ☐ No
10 During this tax year, did you sell or dispose of the like-kind property you received? . . . . ☐ Yes ☐ No
   *If both lines 9 and 10 are "No," go to Part II. If either line 9 or line 10 is "Yes," the deferred gain or (loss) from line 24 must
   be reported on your return this tax year, **unless** one of the exceptions on line 11 applies. See instructions.*
11 If one of the exceptions below applies to the disposition, check the applicable box:
   a ☐ The disposition was after the death of either of the related parties.
   b ☐ The disposition was an involuntary conversion, and the threat of conversion occurred after the exchange.
   c ☐ You can establish to the satisfaction of the IRS that neither the exchange nor the disposition had tax avoidance as
       its principal purpose. If this box is checked, attach an explanation. See instructions.

Part II   Realized Gain or (Loss), Recognized Gain, and Basis of Like-Kind Property Received

Caution: *If you transferred and received (a) more than one group of like-kind properties, or (b) cash or other (not like-kind)
property, see instructions under Multi-Asset Exchanges.*

Note: *Complete lines 12 through 14 ONLY if you gave up property that was not like-kind. Otherwise, go to line 15.*

12 Fair market value (FMV) of other property given up . . . . . . | **12** |
13 Adjusted basis of other property given up . . . . | **13** |
14 Gain or (loss) recognized on other property given up. Subtract line 13 from line 12. Report the
   gain or (loss) in the same manner as if the exchange had been a sale . . . . | **14** |
15 Cash received, FMV of other property received, plus net liabilities assumed by other party, reduced
   (but not below zero) by any exchange expenses you incurred. See instructions . . . . . . | **15** |
16 FMV of like-kind property you received . . . . | **16** |
17 Add lines 15 and 16 . . . . | **17** |
18 Adjusted basis of like-kind property you gave up, net amounts paid to other party, plus any
   exchange expenses **not** used on line 15. See instructions . . . . | **18** |
19 **Realized gain or (loss).** Subtract line 18 from line 17 . . . . | **19** |
20 Enter the smaller of line 15 or line 19, but not less than zero . . . . | **20** |
21 Ordinary income under recapture rules. Enter here and on Form 4797, line 17. See instructions | **21** |
22 Subtract line 21 from line 20. If zero or less, enter -0-. If more than zero, enter here and on Schedule
   D or Form 4797, unless the installment method applies. See instructions . . . . | **22** |
23 **Recognized gain.** Add lines 21 and 22 . . . . | **23** |
24 Deferred gain or (loss). Subtract line 23 from line 19. If a related party exchange, see instructions . | **24** |
25 **Basis of like-kind property received.** Subtract line 15 from the sum of lines 18 and 23 . . | **25** |

For Paperwork Reduction Act Notice, see separate instructions.   Cat. No. 12311A   Form **8824** (1992)

355

Figure C-10. Form 8824.

Form 8824 (1992)   Page **2**

Name(s) shown on tax return. Do not enter name and social security number if shown on other side.	Your social security number

Part III Section 1043 Conflict-of-Interest Sales. See instructions. Attach a copy of your certificate of divestiture.

Note: *This part is only to be used by officers or employees of the executive branch of the Federal Government for reporting nonrecognition of gain under section 1043 on the sale of property to comply with the conflict-of-interest requirements. This part can be used only if the cost of the replacement property exceeds the basis of the divested property.*

26 Description of divested property ▶ ....

27 Description of replacement property ▶ ....

28 Date divested property was sold (month, day, year) . . . . **28** / /

29 Sales price of divested property. See instructions . . . . . . | **29** |

30 Basis of divested property . . . . | **30** |

31 **Realized gain.** Subtract line 30 from line 29 . . . . **31**

32 Cost of replacement property purchased within 60 days after date of sale . . . . | **32** |

33 Subtract line 32 from line 29. If zero or less, enter -0- **33**

34 Ordinary income under recapture rules. Enter here and on Form 4797, line 11. See instructions **34**

35 Subtract line 34 from line 33. If zero or less, enter -0-. If more than zero, enter here and on Schedule D or Form 4797. See instructions **35**

36 **Recognized gain.** Add lines 34 and 35 . . . . **36**

37 Deferred gain. Subtract line 36 from line 31 . . . . **37**

38 **Basis of replacement property.** Subtract line 37 from line 32 . . . . **38**

Form **8829**	Expenses for Business Use of Your Home	OMB No. 1545-1266
Department of the Treasury Internal Revenue Service (X)	▶ File with Schedule C (Form 1040). Use a separate Form 8829 for each home you used for business during the year. ▶ See instructions on back.	19**92** Attachment Sequence No. **66**

Name(s) of proprietor(s)   Your social security number

Part I   Part of Your Home Used for Business

1 Area used exclusively for business (see instructions). Include area that does not meet exclusive use test and either used for inventory storage or regularly used as part of a day-care facility   **1**
2 Total area of home   **2**
3 Divide line 1 by line 2. Enter the result as a percentage   **3**   %
   • For day-care facilities not used exclusively for business, also complete lines 4-6.
   • All others, skip lines 4-6 and enter the amount from line 3 on line 7.
4 Multiply days used for day care during year by hours used per day   **4**   hr.
5 Total hours available for use during the year (366 days × 24 hours). See instructions   **5**   8,784 hr.
6 Divide line 4 by line 5. Enter the result as a decimal amount   **6**
7 Business percentage. For day-care facilities not used exclusively for business, multiply line 6 by line 3 (enter the result as a percentage). All others, enter the amount from line 3   ▶   **7**   %

Part II   ure Your Allowable Deduction

8 Enter the   nt from Schedule C, line 29, **plus** any net gain or (loss) derived from the business use of your home and shown on Schedule D or Form 4797. If more than one place of business, see instructions   **8**

See instructions for columns (a) and (b) before completing lines 9-20. | (a) Direct expenses | (b) Indirect expenses |

9   Casualty losses. See instructions   **9**
10 Deductible mortgage interest. See instructions   **10**
11 Real estate taxes. See instructions   **11**
12 Add lines 9, 10, and 11   **12**
13 Multiply line 12, column (b) by line 7   **13**
14 Add line 12, column (a) and line 13   **14**
15 Subtract line 14 from line 8. If zero or less, enter -0-   **15**
16 Excess mortgage interest. See instructions   **16**
17 Insurance   **17**
18 Repairs and maintenance   **18**
19 Utilities   **19**
20 Other expenses. See   structions   **20**
21 Add lines 16 through   **21**
22 Multiply line 21, colum   b) by line 7   **22**
23 Carryover of operating expenses from 1991 Form 8829, line 41   **23**
24 Add line 21 in column (a), line 22, and line 23   **24**
25 Allowable operating expenses. Enter the **smaller** of line 15 or line 24   **25**
26 Limit on excess casualty losses and depreciation. Subtract line 25 from line 15   **26**
27 Excess casualty losses. See instructions   **27**
28 Depreciation of your home from Part III below   **28**
29 Carryover of excess casualty losses and depreciation from 1991 Form 8829, line 42   **29**
30 Add lines 27 through 29   **30**
31 Allowable excess casualty losses and depreciation. Enter the **smaller** of line 26 or line 30   **31**
32 Add lines 14, 25, and 31   **32**
33 Casualty loss portion, if any, from lines 14 and 31. Carry amount to **Form 4684**, Section B   **33**
34 Allowable expenses for business use of your home. Subtract line 33 from line 32. Enter here and on Schedule C, line 30. If your home was used for more than one business, see instructions ▶   **34**

Part III   Depreciation of Your Home

35 Enter the **smaller** of your home's adjusted basis or its fair market value. See instructions   **35**
36 Value of land included on line 35   **36**
37 Basis of building. Subtract line 36 from line 35   **37**
38 Business basis of building. Multiply line 37 by line 7   **38**
39 Depreciation percentage. See instructions   **39**   %
40 Depreciation allowable. Multiply line 38 by line 39. Enter here and on line 28 above. See instructions   **40**

Part IV   Carryover of Unallowed Expenses to 1993

41 Operating expenses. Subtract line 25 from line 24. If less than zero, enter -0-   **41**
42 Excess casualty losses and depreciation. Subtract line 31 from line 30. If less than zero, enter -0-   **42**

For Paperwork Reduction Act Notice, see back of form.   Cat. No. 13232M   Form **8829** (1992)

359

Figure C-11. Form 8829.

Index

About the Authors

ROBERT IRWIN has been a successful real estate broker for more than 25 years and has steered countless buyers, sellers, and beginning investors through every kind of real estate transaction imaginable. He has served as a consultant to lenders, investors, and other brokers and is one of the most knowledgeable and prolific writers in the field. His books include *Tips and Traps When Buying a Home, Tips and Traps When Selling a Home,* and *Tips and Traps When Mortgage Hunting.*

NORMAN H. LANE is a partner in the national and international law firm of Bryan Cave, where he heads the west coast tax practice. Formerly of the faculty of USC's Law Center in Los Angeles, he is well known for his writing on tax and estate planning subjects.